The View from the Barrio

The View
from
the Barrio

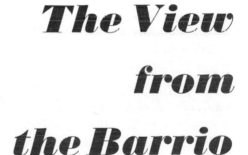

by Lisa Redfield Peattie

Ann Arbor Paperbacks
The University of Michigan Press

Dedicado a:
Ali, Marcos, Trina, Tomás, Felicia, Jorge, Hortensia—y todos los
demás habitantes del Barrio La Laja, haciendo el futuro con sus
proprias vidas.

Second printing 1972
First edition as an Ann Arbor Paperback 1970
Copyright © by The University of Michigan 1968
All rights reserved
ISBN 0-472-06169-0
Published in the United States of America by
The University of Michigan Press and
in Don Mills, Canada, by Longman Canada Limited
Manufactured in the United States of America

Acknowledgments

This book is a result of two and a half years as anthropologist with a team of planners in Venezuela. In February 1962 my husband and I went to work—he as architect, I as anthropologist—in a project of the Harvard-MIT Joint Center for Urban Studies, under contract with the Venezuelan government to help plan a new industrial city. What I did in Venezuela was neither social action, except as a human being with other human beings acts and interacts, nor was it research in the conventional sense, for I had no "problem," no "research design." I was trying to find out what an anthropologist could learn and say that would contribute to planning in that situation. I left Venezuela in July 1964. The Joint Center for Urban Studies gave me the year that followed to think and write about what I had seen and for that year I owe thanks.

I am grateful also to a number of individuals for reading parts of this account in manuscript and giving me suggestions. Among those who gave me their time in this way were: Lloyd Rodwin, John Thorkelson, Alexander Ganz, Jose Antonio Rangel, Peter Eckstein, Jaleel Ahmad, Mary Lou Munts, David Gutmann, and David Fairchild. I did not always take the suggestions they gave, and for what is here said, I alone wish to be held accountable.

RIO ORIN

LAGUNA ACAPULCO

Puerto Ordaz

RIO CARONI

Photograph by Tranarg C. A., Caracas, Venezuela.

Contents

Todos se han quedado contentos
con presentaciones siniestras
de rápidos capitalistas
y sistemáticas mujeres.
Yo quiero hablar con muchas cosas . . .

—Pablo Neruda, *Bestiario*

1.
Introduction

Anthropologists have a notable tendency to think small. Setting out to describe China, they tell us about the village of Yit s'un; modern Japan is looked at from the rice fields of the village of Suye Mura. So, if an anthropologist reports on a large economic development and urban-planning project in a country undergoing rapid economic and political change by recounting how things are in one very small working-class barrio of a developing city, she has at least the excuse of precedent.

The following pages, then, attempt to describe what is going on in La Laja, an urban neighborhood—what the Latin Americans call a barrio—in a rapidly growing, planned city in the interior of Venezuela. Supposing that what is happening in La Laja is neither unique nor isolated, and trying to understand what is to be seen in terms of the connections which seem to appear between La Laja's life processes and elements of the surrounding environment, the attempt is made to come to some understanding of the surrounding environment, as a new city, as Venezuela, or as one of the typical developing countries.

There is at times an element of the ridiculous in this procedure, like a child trying to understand a dinner party by sitting under the table. But there is something to be said for it as well. The conceptualizers and planners have to operate on a large scale: the scale of maps of regional economic flows, of migration statistics, of predictions on labor force need and supply. But in the end, all these generalizations and plans are summaries of what individual human beings are doing with themselves or will be doing in the future. It sometimes helps, even for the general planner, to look at what his plans and generalizations mean on a small scale, the scale of the individual human being or the single neighborhood. The planner may also find it most useful to look at what is happening outside, inside, and around his plans and his control. This is an attempt to take such a look at some large-scale social processes from the bottom, working out from a single small case. It might be called an ethnography of urbanization and economic development.

The 1930 opera of Kurt Weill and Bertolt Brecht, *The Rise and Fall of the City of Mahagonny,* begins with the founding of a city by chance—by individuals whose particular life histories have brought them together at a certain place and time. Three fugitives from justice are traveling along a coast toward some gold fields when their truck breaks down. Unable to proceed further, they set up a gaming table under a tree, hang out a rag on a fishing rod to attract the attention of passing sailors and gold prospectors, and declare Mahagonny, the "city of nets" founded—a commercial center to catch the earnings of men.

Very different was the official founding of the city of which Barrio La Laja is a part. For this barrio is part of the city of Ciudad Guayana in the interior of Venezuela, at the point where the Caroní River joins the Orinoco. This city was formally founded in 1961 as a planned industrial city, its official inauguration celebrated by a well-publicized ceremonial in which many prominent persons took part, its further development under the charge of the Corporación Venezolana de Guayana, an autonomous agency of the Venezuelan government. Instead of a poker table, this city had as its nucleus a new steel mill and a dam and electric power plant, both government-owned and already managed by the Corporación, as well as two private mining companies (subsidiaries of U. S. Steel and Bethlehem Steel) and an existing nucleus of settlement of almost 50,000 people. Nor was this city, like Mahagonny of the opera, to grow as a city of uncontrolled individualism— *"frischen Fleischsalat und keine Direktion,"* in the words of Brecht's libretto. This city was to be planned and developed by the Corporación de Guayana in accordance with the national economic targets set for the country as a whole and was to contribute to national goals; the Corporación was given very wide powers in the control of land so as to be able to shape the form of the city. This city was to be a corporate artifact, consciously created.

The Venezuelan government planners were soon joined by a group of American consultants from the Joint Center for Urban Studies of the Massachusetts Institute of Technology and Harvard. The city's future was planned in more detail. The economists of the team began to project possible industrial bases of the new city, basing these projections on the available resources in high-grade iron ore and other minerals, cheap hydroelectric power, nearby oil and gas, and ocean transport down the Orinoco. They began to work out what this sort of base might mean in terms of population— 250,000 by 1970, they said, well over 600,000 by 1980. They tried to project the ways in which the economic structure of the population on the site would change as the city and its industries grew. Meanwhile, the urban designers drew plans of urban form and considered the transportation patterns and the patterns of commerce, industry, and residence which the new city should have.

The government of Venezuela was developing a new industrial center in the country's interior, three hundred miles from the parts of the country already densely populated. It was building a city at the confluence of the Orinoco and Caroní rivers. It was making a social and economic transformation of the Guayana as part of a planned economic transformation of the nation as a whole.

But the city of Ciudad Guayana is also a Mahagonny, a confluence of the life histories, of the particular needs, of many individuals who came there, and who will come there, not as part of "a plan" but in following life paths leading to this place for private reasons. It is not only that well over 40,000 people were living at the city site when the official inauguration took place in 1961— some of them having lived there for twenty years. It is not merely that there was in the older town nucleus a municipal government, a Catholic parish, a Rotary Club, a Chamber of Commerce—all of these also being actors in the growth of the city. It is also that even as the city grows under the planners' stimulus and direction, it grows only partly according to plan; it grows also as a Mahagonny. It is a part of planning to realize this.

The planners have a number of points of control to shape the future development of Ciudad Guayana, but in the end they come to much the same as the placing of the poker table of Mahagonny under a tree and hanging out an old rag on a fishing rod. In these two founding acts of Weill's opera are seen in germinal form three of the main points at which the Corporación can shape the development of that city: capital investment, the locating of institutions, and promotion. In addition, the Corporación has done some stimulating of educational facilities at various levels—from technical training down to community classes in sewing and cooking. But here, too, the principle is the same. People will come to the planned city because it attracts them. They will use the city and its industry and its institutions in ways that they see they are to be used, although these things may in the end be remade by the life the people make there.

One of the chief subjects of the following pages concerns the way in which some people are using Ciudad Guayana, the life paths which brought them there, and the paths which they are threading through an urban-industrial environment which is not only new, but is still in process of creation. It is an environment within which, and in terms of which, people are transforming themselves. These processes of change—from one point of view called social mobility; from another, cultural change; from another, social change—are a chief focus of what follows.

The other chief subject of what follows is, necessarily, the nature of the environment with reference to which individuals are becoming changed and which, in turn, they are continually re-creating in altered form. Men continually shape their social and economic world, but their social and economic world shapes them. Every man's life design and every group's set of social forms and conventional behaviors and values involve coping with a set of circumstances largely outside their immediate control. Every way of life exists in terms of a set of parameters. Even Brecht finds it necessary to explain his Mahagonny in terms of the cities, the lumber camps, the gold fields, which make up its outer world; and the plot of the opera is the story of what Mahagonny, a city as nearly ruleless as human life can be, does to its residents. So the kinds of individual and social transformation going on in Ciudad Guayana can only be understood in terms of their economic and social parameters, and these then become a part of our subject.

In describing the nature of these parameters, the environment within which people find their ways, a dual theme emerges. This theme is that of Venezuela—an underdeveloped society with a developed society's technology. Venezuela is in truth an underdeveloped country, but one which is underdeveloped in a curiously uneven way. Venezuela is relatively rich, with the highest per capita income in Latin America; it is second only to the United

States and Canada in the New World. With its riches it has bought itself the vestments of the modern world, from steel mills and clover-leaf highway interchanges down to a vast range of consumer goods for the common man. Yet inside these vestments, the transformation to a developed economy's systems of organization and motivation is still far from complete.

The result is a curious mixture of extremes: great national wealth, with a mass of very poor people; superhighways next to which people carry on traditional corn-patch agriculture or marginal forms of trade and wage labor; people who believe in witchcraft, for whom Pepsi-Cola is a dietary staple, and whose women do their hair on roller curlers in imitation of the latest New York fashions.

Two general aspects of this curious mixture deserve comment. One is what appears to be a general deficiency in social organization, based on a still-incomplete transformation of a traditional Latin-American status order. In all Venezuelan institutions there appears to be a gap between the top levels and the bottom, a weakness in structure at the intermediate levels. It is no doubt a cause for national self-congratulation that—as the president of Venezuela pointed out in the midst of the 1963 preelection terrorism the Communists in Venezuela have very little of a mass base. But this fact appears in a less favorable light when it may be claimed that the same is true of other political parties, and of most national agencies and institutions. From this structural circumstance it follows that besides the natural tendency for the country's wealth to be concentrated at the top national government levels—in the form of oil revenues—there is a notable weakness in the bureaucratic structures for distributing this wealth downward, in the form of general economic development, education, and the like. Equally, when the structure is viewed by the man at the bottom there is a corresponding deficiency in mechanisms for those at the bottom to press their needs to those in control, or to advance themselves upward through some sort of step-by-step mobility ladder. One of the themes of what follows will be the routes and connections between those at the bottom, in La Laja, and those at the top.

Another aspect of the rich underdeveloped society relevant to our theme of individual lifeways is related both to the absolute wealth present in the society and to the spread of communications—roads, radios, newspapers, and widespread marketing of goods—which that wealth has supported and which makes it visible. This is a transformation of aspirations. This is a society in which people live in full knowledge of a tremendous range of goods—automobiles, clothes, refrigerators, educations and the like—and aspire to possess them. Meanwhile, the distribution of such goods is notably uneven, and the institutional mechanisms for equalizing distribution are still developing. The result is a gap, potentially explosive, between aspiration and acquisition, between "want" and "get." The people of La Laja are committed to what the developed economy can provide, but they are still not fully able to get the developed economy to deliver for them.

In looking at life in La Laja, in seeing how new migrants to the industrial city make their lives in it, still another set of considerations emerges. We ask how moving into a modern industrial economy affects people in La Laja—how well, how fast they are learning to live in the new world. And the question seems to bring not one answer but two. People are learning to be industrial workers faster than one might expect, but people seem to be learning ways of living and being which are in some sense disfunctional for building a future in the modern industrialized economy. Things are getting better very fast, but in some ways they are also, through the same processes, getting worse. The better may more than compensate for the worse, but it seems worthwhile to look at both aspects.

In any case, La Laja is part of a city, part of a region, part of a nation, part of a world which is rapidly transforming itself. The scene of the story is part of a planned and, at the same time, spontaneously developing city in an unevenly developed society. People are migrating to this city at a rate which multiplies the population by ten each decade; and in this setting the migrants are becoming different sorts of people as, simultaneously, using and making the city, they remake the environment while it remakes them.

This theme has a name—economic development. I believe these changes in people and in their social environment are more than consequences or peripheral aspects of the economic development process—they are the stuff of which economic development is made, or the process itself on its smallest scale. If so, it may be possible to derive generalizations about the process in general from this one small instance. The pages which follow are in part a methodological exercise, an attempt to see what the view from little Barrio La Laja can suggest about the major historical transformation in which Venezuela is caught up.

2.
The View from La Laja

When I came back to Ciudad Guayana in the Venezuelan interior
after being away for nine months, I felt almost overwhelmed by a
sensation to which, when I lived there for two-and-a-half years, I
had become so accustomed I had forgotten it: the violence of that
urban setting. A city has grown in fourteen years from 4000 to
about 50,000 people at the southern edge of the great dry grass-
and-chaparral plains of Venezuela. It is eight degrees off the equa-
tor and nearly at sea level, the sky seems extraordinarily wide and
clear and pours down light and heat. The wide Orinoco River and
the more rocky Caroní, which rushes from the south to fall over a
magnificent waterfall and run into the Orinoco at the city site,
interrupt but do not temper the land. Under that wide sky's bowl
of light the new roads and new concrete buildings—rows of developer houses, apartment buildings, commercial structures—seem
to erupt from the dust-dry earth which bulldozers have scraped
clear of vegetation. Elsewhere, the improvised housing of the poor,
of sheet aluminum or pressed-board, looks as if it had been thrown
together by a hurricane. It is a city of bulldozers, of engineers who
wear boots and dungarees and carry shiny briefcases, of noisy bars
and holes in the streets, and of new traffic interchanges; it is a city
of building and of disorderly entrepreneurship; it is a city which
lives in the future.

I began again to be intoxicated by that atmosphere and to realize how, without knowing it, I had been missing it, as at the same time I remembered that we had chosen to live in that neighborhood of the city called Barrio La Laja as a way of escaping some of its force. We had four children, and we came to live in La Laja because it looked more settled than many other parts of the city, and because its scale as a community seemed of a dimension for children to handle—children who had the language to learn, as well as a new way of living. La Laja, at twenty years of settlement, is an old neighborhood, as antiquity goes in Ciudad Guayana; it has natural boundaries which separate it from the rest of the city; it has less than five hundred people. Its tightly-packed, brightly-painted houses along dirt streets suggest "village" rather than "city." I think this must be said at the outset because in the pages which follow I intend to talk from that base—one case, one place, a small, well-established working-class barrio, where for two years I lived with my family in a house with earth walls and a sheet-aluminum roof.

The map of the city tacked on my wall there showed Barrio La Laja clearly as a triangular settlement bounded on one side by the property line—marked by a steel fence—of the Iron Mines Company of Venezuela, and on the other two by contour lines, representing the annual high-water level of the Orinoco. One side of the triangle faces the river itself. The other contour line represents a sort of flood plain or lagoon which nearly laps the dirt road from the highway in the rainy season, and which in the dry season is covered with wild vegetation and a few patches of corn. The site is, in effect, a flat shelf of rock, or *laja*, for which the barrio was named.

Our house faced the Orinoco. At the end of the rainy season the river was within a few feet of the cement extension which ran along the housefront. By the end of the dry season the river had dropped forty feet, and a broad beach of white sand stretched between the house and the water. There was usually something to look at out there. Large ore boats of the Orinoco Mining Company (a U. S. Steel subsidiary) and Iron Mines Company (Bethlehem Steel) passed up and down the river, as did dugout canoes, each with an American-made outboard motor. At regular intervals one could see the little launch which carried commuting workers from the town center of San Félix, which I could see just downstream, to the industrial area of Puerto Ordaz, just out of sight around a bend upstream. Once in a while the beach of La Laja would be the stopping-place for a launch from the regional capital of Ciudad

Bolívar, further upstream, or from the town downstream at the entrance to the delta. Women at the edge of the river beat dirty clothes on the rocks, on an abandoned car body at the edge of the river, or on an old wooden table set in the water. Children and young men dived and swam. The ore boats and the women beating their wash with sticks, the dugout canoes with outboard motors—in the view from my front door seemed to be a juxtaposition of images which said something about what was happening in Ciudad Guayana.

The people of La Laja, by and large, did not think of themselves as living in Ciudad Guayana, and few other residents of the city did either. "The city" as a whole was, in effect, still to be created; what existed was a series of separate settlements strung out along eighteen miles of highway between the town of San Félix and the new steel mill.

The easternmost of these settlements, and the one with the largest population, was the town of San Félix. Before the mining companies came to the region, the first in the 1940's, the second in the 1950's, San Félix had been a little river port of less than 2000 persons, laid out in the traditional Latin style with a gridwork of streets around the central plaza with its bust of Simon Bolívar in the middle. The Catholic church was at one side of the plaza and the offices of the municipal government, a dependency of the district government in Upata to the south, were at the other; the market was in a disorderly series of booths along the river. There was one doctor and a few general stores.

The inrush of population brought about by the arrival of the iron mining companies and the building of the dam and power plant added to this central nucleus a series of barrios—satellite residential areas—with more meandering street patterns and brought the population to something like 40,000 people in the 1960's; in the one year after the dictatorship fell in 1958 and controls on building were temporarily suspended, about a thousand houses went up east of the plaza alone. This growth had also added a rush of commercial entrepreneurship—the Lebanese, mostly in clothing and cloth, the Italians and Spaniards, in hardware, foods, and other goods, tailors from Trinidad, a few Chinese bakers and restaurant owners. The tone of the town was set by the commercial elite, who expressed their interests politically through the chamber of commerce and the municipal government, and dominated its social life through the Rotary Club, Masons, and the Shooting Club.

Of the barrios of San Félix, La Laja was one. The central plaza of San Félix was "the plaza" for the people of La Laja, and the church beside it was "the church." The jail on the other side was where they were taken when they were arrested; the municipal offices were where they went to dicker for a license to sell beer, to ask for materials to build a neighborhood water line, or to apply for emergency charity.

The iron mining companies also brought two company "camps," each with an industrial area for preliminary processing and loading and its company-built worker housing, schools, and community facilities. The "camp" of the Iron Mines Company on the San Félix side of the river was small, since that company had its main processing operations at the mine to the south. But Puerto Ordaz, the camp of the Orinoco Mining Company across the river, was not only larger—housing about 3000 people—but a dramatically visible enclave of a different style of life. The Americans who lived there were a majority only in what people usually called the "American camp," the area for executive residences around the Country Club at the camp's western edge. But the Americans nevertheless dominated Puerto Ordaz as a whole, which with its modern hospital and other public buildings, its large supermarket, its neat masonry houses, and its green lawns, was a visible image of the power and competence of the North American development model. It was so experienced by people from La Laja who went there to work for the company, to shop in its stores, to visit friends and kinsmen in its worker housing, or to work as domestic servants in the homes of "the Americans." The power of the image—of richness, of strength, of "order" in physical arrangements and in family life—was, of course, strengthened by the circumstance that the "company" had exported to Venezuela only that middle-class suburban way of life which is America's pre-eminent creation; poverty, disease, old age, urban disorder had all been left behind, as had the turbulent nineteenth-century history of political and industrial development which had at last eventuated in this product.

The sharpness of the Puerto Ordaz image could only gain by the crowded, disorderly jumble of commerce and residence lining the road which connected the camp with the ferry landing at the Caroní and thus, eventually, with San Félix. For here all that explosive individual enterprise which did not fit within the company framework, but which stood to profit by the new center of activity and income which the company represented, had tried to squeeze itself into the limited available space outside the company property. The social ingredients here were much the same as in San Félix—commercial entrepreneurs, largely immigrant to Venezuela, in addition to a great heterogeneous mass of in-migrating job-seekers—but here they appeared in a speculative jockeying for place in a narrow area, undisciplined by the urban institutions of San Félix proper. On the other side of the river, at the ferry boat landing on the San Félix side of the water, was a settlement similar in character but with somewhat less commercial vitality, representing the growing edge of the city's life of a few years earlier.

The city thus presented itself as growing around several sharply contrasted poles of force. The first was a local commercial elite with personal cultural connections with Europe, and political connections through Ciudad Bolívar to Caracas. The second pole was represented by the American companies, the source of much of the regional road-building and other infrastructure and also of the hard core of industrial jobs which were the economic basis of the city—including the commercial life around which its local elite had formed.

A third pole was represented by the various activities of the Corporación Venezolana de Guayana, the national government's regional development corporation. This pole was somewhat more complex. "The Corporation" was another sort of company, or rather two companies: the small enterprise represented by the dam and power plant on the Caroní, with its little company "camp," and the much larger one represented by the new integrated steel mill at the western edge of the urban complex. However, "the Corporation" was responsible not only for developing special housing for steel mill employees, like any company, but for general urban planning and development. Thus, it was decided not to build another "company camp" but to combine the steel mill housing with the existing urban structure, mainly around Puerto Ordaz; furthermore, the Corporation began to organize various urbanizations for ordinary persons in the city, not employees of the CVG, and to run small-scale social services in them. On both sides of the river various housing developments appeared, each quite distinct in physical form and in the social characteristics of the residents and dependent on a center of power quite distinct from either the American companies or the local government. Working from Caracas, the Corporation also strove to attract new industries to the region. The development corporation thus represented a number of things: jobs and mobility possibilities, like any company, a source of roads and public services, and new styles of urbanizing. Less visibly to the people of La Laja, the Corporation was also a stimulus to economic development in the area. For the people of La Laja, all three of these centers were possible sources of individual jobs and of assistance to the community. For example, when members of the barrio organized to build a center at which children would get a daily free breakfast provided by the state, the development corporation, the municipal government, and one of the mining companies were all tapped for tools and materials.

In this complex urban world, La Laja is socially defined as a *barrio bajo,* a distinctively lower-class neighborhood. That we Americans lived there, and the occasional residence in the barrio of other middle-class elements—a Lebanese hardware dealer, a Corporación de Guayana social worker—was not sufficient to change this clear class identification. This was true even though there were in the city no distinctively middle-class neighborhoods outside the company "camps" and none of the *gente buena* lived far away from people of lower social status. But to the *gente buena* there is a difference between living in San Félix next to poor people and living in a place like La Laja. They tended to be intrigued and a little upset by our living there with our children; they expressed concern over my children's having "nobody" for friends (there were, of course, several hundred children in the barrio) and worried about "what might happen" to my eldest daughter in such a place. They tended to try to understand my presence in the barrio as part of some ill-defined charitable enterprise: "doing good work there."

So what follows, dealing largely with processes of social mobility and incipient class differentiation within the barrio, must be understood in the light of one clear preliminary fact: all these processes are taking place at a social level still separated by a considerable gap from the *gente buena* or established middle class.

La Laja came into existence as a settlement of wage laborers for the Iron Mines Company of Venezuela, clustered next to the fence shutting off company property and along the original road between the company camp and San Félix. By now, only a small number of residents work for the Iron Mines Company, and many of its earlier founders have moved elsewhere. Of the two hundred adults in the barrio, about 22 percent had lived there less than a year at the time of study, and another quarter had been living there between one and five years. Still in the barrio, however, was a core of long-term residents; 15 percent of the barrio's adults had lived there sixteen years or more—almost from its inception—and another 22 percent from eleven to fifteen years. The first family to arrive was still living there.

Of all the barrio's residents, only nine adults had been born in Ciudad Guayana. Another fifteen came from the regional capital, Ciudad Bolívar, just up the river. The largest part of the barrio's people (about 30 percent) had come from the delta of the Orinoco or the towns adjoining the delta. Another fifth had come from the oil, mining, and cattle state of Anzoátegui just to the north. About a tenth came from the mountainous, rural state of Sucre along the northern coast of Venezuela. The barrio included (besides us Americans) one foreign-born man, an Arab cloth dealer married to a Venezuelan woman. When censused, it also included one family recently arrived from Caracas, who soon moved out to a site in one of the new Corporación de Guayana subdivisions. There were five men from the Island of Margarita off the northern coast, but except for the Caraqueños there was no one from the Andean region where most of Venezuela's people live. In this pattern of geographic origins the barrio again reflects its position in the class structure. This is a city in which much of the commercial class comes from Europe or the Middle East, in which technical and managerial people come from Caracas or the Andes (if not from the United States or Italy) and the lower class is drawn predominantly from the rural areas of eastern Venezuela.

When I made my census in 1962, La Laja had 490 inhabitants, living in eighty household groups. Of the 490, 123 were under seven years of age, and another 106 under thirteen. Children under thirteen thus comprised nearly half the population. Teenagers (thirteen to eighteen inclusive) were another 13 percent. Persons over fifty were only 6 percent of the total—and even so, a higher proportion than for the city as a whole. The sex ratio was about balanced at all age levels.

The barrio of La Laja consists physically of three uneven-shaped blocks of small one-story houses separated by two wide unpaved streets. Since the limited, triangular site on which these houses are built limits the length of the two main streets and causes them to taper slightly in width, and since trees and buildings block a view through at the east end of each, these two main streets serve, if not quite as plazas, at least as semi-enclosed public spaces. Both are used for parking cars and trucks, of which there are likely to be a half dozen in the barrio at normal times. The larger of the two streets has the two-classroom school building at one end and the old school, converted into a community center, at the other, which also contains the court for bowling, built in 1962 by two Americans as part of a community development project. In the same area is the asphalted volleyball court, built by the community. On the other street a vacant lot has been made into a small playground for children by a local storekeeper and one of his friends; the play equipment consists of a merry-go-round made out of scavenged wheels set in concrete. Next to this playground is the "children's breakfast center," a recent community building project, in which the state provides a daily free meal to about fifty children.

As part of the 1962 community development project, trees were planted in these public spaces. Aside from this touch of green and a few older trees, the people of La Laja strive for the effect in their public spaces as in their own yards of neatly-swept earth. When feeling energetic and civic-minded, they may be seen pulling out the grass which springs up in patches during the rains. There are a few denser and more established patches of grass, and to deal with these a group of men bought a small power mower. Those who feel inclined sweep the streets, especially the part nearest their houses. City trash collection was introduced in La Laja during my residence, and barrels for trash were provided by one of the companies, but this system has not yet completely supplanted the older method of getting rid of trash by throwing it on the beach or in the brush beside the road to the highway.

There are in the barrio nine public water sources, each consisting of two faucets mounted on a cement block. These were installed by the people of the barrio in 1962 and bring chlorinated water by a small pipeline from the water tower in the larger neighboring barrio of El Roble. Water is usually turned on for only a few hours in the day; there were often days when no water came at all.

Sewage runs off toward river or lagoon in earth channels which in a few places have been lined with cement. When the channels become clogged, the residents of adjacent houses sometimes clear them out with a spade.

Streets other than the two main ones and the entrance road are rough with rocks. All are of earth. The entrance road is periodically scraped by the Iron Mines Company; the others are left to the community. From time to time during my stay, the barrio negotiated with the municipal government to try to have the streets asphalted.

When studied, La Laja had ninety-two buildings under construction or in good enough condition to be inhabited. Seventy-four of these were being lived in, seven were under construction, six were empty, three were used only for business, and two more were public buildings—one the new school, the other the community center. Four of the dwelling houses were divided into two or three apartments. Because of the natural limitations on expansion in the barrio there are buildings on most of the available land. The main streets are lined with houses abutting each on the next. A vacant piece of land generally is so because someone is believed to have a claim on it (usually by having built there at one time) which he is not currently exercising; such claims to land are not legal, the land being in public ownership, but by custom are respected.

Houses in La Laja are constructed of one of the two main building materials: cement blocks or *bahareque*—earth mixed with manure and straw. (There is one exception to this: a small shack built out of boards and scrap built out along the sands at the far edge of the barrio and belonging to an Indian with a Negroid wife. This family, which lives mainly by the husband's fishing, is at the bottom of La Laja's rudimentary social ladder.) Of these two materials, *bahareque* represents the traditional and rural, cement blocks the more modern and urban. The cement block houses are universally esteemed as the better of the two. Houses built originally out of *bahareque* may be rebuilt in cement block by building the new walls around or inside the old, and then removing the *bahareque*. This process can be seen going on a good deal of the time. The first cement block house was built in La Laja ten years ago; by now, over a third of the dwellings are cement block.

A *bahareque* house is built by putting up a framework of heavy posts and beams and then tacking thin poles, or more often bamboo, horizontally across the wall area about three inches apart. The wall is then plastered with a mixture of mud, straw, and manure. The most rudimentary version leaves the house at this stage, but most houses in La Laja are then plastered with whitish clay from the river bottom. This is usually whitewashed, either in white or in colors. The base of the walls, inside and out, is painted in a strip of a darker color. Doors and window shutters are invariably painted a different color from the walls. Color combinations are vivid, varied, and tasteful.

The cement block house is not only built according to a different principle of construction (supporting walls, rather than posts and beams) but also in style generally follows a different model from the house of *bahareque*. Instead of having a pitched roof overhanging the walls like the *bahareque* house, it presents a vertical facade with a decorative upper edging, often scalloped or ornamented in relief. These decorations are emphasized by color in the painting. Such a house may have, although this is not standard in La Laja, a small front porch or garden. Another desired touch of elegance is aluminum grillwork over the windows. Such a house is a *quintica* or poor man's imitation of the rich man's garden-surrounded *quinta*.

There were still eleven houses with thatched roofs in La Laja. Thatch is relatively cool and does not reverberate during the heavy rains, but is being replaced by sheet aluminum for cleanliness, freedom from insects, easy upkeep, and general modernity by everyone who can afford to make the shift. Surely, there would never be a thatched roof on a cement block house.

Even the *bahareque* house in La Laja typically had a cement floor. Workmanship on these floors is good; they present a slick surface usually mopped daily with immense sloshing of water. The kitchen, conceived by the people of La Laja as a work space with few "presentation" aspects, and generally located at the rear, more often has an earth floor. While only thirteen houses had earth floors in the house proper, thirty-seven had earth floors in the kitchen.

Of the houses in the barrio censused by the Ministry of Health in 1962, less than a quarter were classified as having adequate outhouses, and over half had none at all. Residents of the latter used the yard, or more typically the woods between the barrio and the Iron Mines Settlement. The Ministry of Health was carrying on a program for building outhouses with donated materials under supervision, but even this did not result in supplying the whole barrio.

One house in La Laja, recently built, has glass in the windows. The school also has glass windows. Other houses have unglazed window openings closed at night or when privacy is desired (an open window is an invitation to peer in) by wooden shutters. Most doors are closed by padlocks rather than standard locks. People in La Laja do not leave their doors unlocked. They say they fear "vagabonds" or boys who are well known to be "terrible" and inclined to carry things off.

All families have at least one fifty-gallon metal drum for water. This is either filled from the public tap, using a hose (the limited number of hoses in the barrio are lent from neighbor to neighbor), or from one of the water trucks which sell water at one bolívar a barrel. Cooking is usually done with kerosene, although two people use bottled gas. Most kerosene stoves are simple two- or three-burner table models, but a few families have elaborate floor models with ovens. Refrigerators are expensive and not general, but are greatly valued.

Most houses have a few fruit trees in back—mangoes, bananas, soursop being the most common—and all have at least some flowering plants, mostly growing in tin cans. There is immense interest in plants among the women. One of the chief elements in social visiting is viewing one another's plants, begging cuttings, and bringing cuttings as gifts. Generally, these are not so much arranged in the form of a garden as set in groups in the back yard and at the front, but some individuals have more elaborate organizations of plants.

Houses, except for the very poorest, have strong "presentation" aspects oriented toward the street or public side. The back yards, fenced with wire or opaque fencing, are a place for outhouses, for washing, and for similar activities, rather than for social interaction with neighbors. The latter takes place most commonly on the paved strip in the front of each house. Here is where, in the cool of the evening, people typically place straight chairs to sit and talk with each other and with passers-by. The front door typically opens into a *sala* or living room, which will be furnished, if economically possible, with a suite of plastic-covered upholstered chairs and a small "coffee table" on which are likely to be reposing plastic flowers in a plaster vase and perhaps a plaster statuette; on the walls hang enlarged photographs of family members, perhaps a picture of the "miraculous doctor," possibly framed photographs of smiling American girls leaning on new motor cars. In the kitchen and more "service"-conceived parts of the house to the rear, the floor is more likely to be earth, and here even a family which can afford plastic-upholstered furniture for the *sala* is likely to use the straight unpainted skin-seated chairs and plain deal tables which are the poor family's furniture. Almost all families in La Laja have at least one veneered bed and wardrobe which serve somewhat the same prestige and image-defining functions as the living-room "set." However, there are often neither beds nor sleeping space for the entire family, the overflow usually being accommodated in hammocks which tend to be hung toward the rear of the dwelling, in the kitchen or yard.

A typical La Laja house thus represents in its physical arrangements a kind of gradient from the more public front to the more private back, which is at the same time a gradient of relative orientation to the urban, commercial economy and to the more traditional and rural. The plastic-upholstered living-room set and the artificial flowers in a plaster vase are part of that same world which women express in their urbanized style of dress and hairdos. The kitchen with its earth floor and deal table heaped with drying dishes, its hammock in the corner, is a residue of that world from which this people is in the process of emergence. The transformation of one into the other has already gone far; for example, in La Laja the large "showpiece" stove is beginning to invade some kitchens, and almost everywhere, even among poorer families, plastic and enamelware have replaced the calabash and hollowed wood tub of the traditional countryside.

But the emergence of La Laja's "worker class" into the urban, commercial, and industrial world is still not complete. One way in which this is expressed in the barrio is in its people's relationship to the natural environment.

The main natural feature of the site is the Orinoco; its seasonal rise and fall, more than the rains, gives La Laja its rhythm of the seasons. The people of La Laja believe their barrio is on an unusually healthful site because of the river; the breeze from the river is cooling and tends to drive away mosquitoes. In a city where obtaining water is a perpetual problem, the river is a source of secure, if muddy, supply, and the clothes-washing site par excellence. Indeed, it is patronized daily by women who walk from considerable distances inland and return carrying their heavy wet clothes in enameled washing pans on their head. However, the people of La Laja do not like to drink river water, and when their supply of clean water (from the water truck or pipeline) runs out, prefer to get drinking water from friends, if possible.

The river is also used for bathing, although not by everyone in the barrio. (Those who do not use the river wash in their houses by pouring water over themselves with a can.) Women generally bathe in an old torn dress, although a couple of younger women have and wear bathing suits. Men wear bathing trunks. Swimming in groups of mixed sex with heterosexual horseplay and lying on the sand in the North American beach style is not practiced by the people of La Laja, although it occasionally is by more "urbanized" types of somewhat higher social class who come to the barrio for its beach.

A good deal of fishing goes on in the river, both from the shore and from dugout canoes. The most common method is by hand-lines, but throw nets and trot lines are also used. Fishing is a masculine occupation. Young girls sometimes fish, but grown women never do. The fish caught are sometimes sold in the barrio or are eaten at home or given to friends. Boys who fish should bring the catch home, but may hold out on the family in order to hold a boys' fish stew feast out in the brush.

The river is generally thought to be dangerous, and with some reason, since it is known to be inhabited by sting rays, alligators, electric eels, and piranhas. Of these menaces, the only common one is the sting ray, which, while it causes about four hours of acute pain, does not cause death. Alligators have been seen near the La Laja beach, and it is said that strong swimmers have been known to drown under mysterious circumstances. Many people in La Laja also believe that under the water is a "skull" which may drag people down.

Even at the time of the full moon when a man or two may come out at night to "catch the fresh air" they usually stay near the houses. People believe that many "vagabonds" walk the beach, especially at night. Children believe that if they play on the beach at night, "vagabonds" may steal them, if not the "headless man" who is supposed to lurk in the bushes at night.

Although the breeze and the river are generally appreciated, even the houses next to the river do not generally face it, but face toward the social life of the street.

Another part of La Laja's natural environment consists of the strip of unimproved land just beyond the Iron Mines fence. This land, covered with brush and cactus, is often used for toileting, especially by children; debris may be dumped there, and children collect certain wild fruits in the brush. Some medicinal plants (from an extensive folk pharmacopeia of herbal remedies) are collected there by adults. Some men of the barrio shoot birds in this piece of monte. Boys hunt birds and sometimes rats with stones, either thrown or projected with a sling shot; their accuracy is astonishing by American standards.

This area of brush is felt at least by children to be a wild and somewhat mysterious place. At night it is said to be haunted by the ghosts of Spaniards murdered by Páez in the Wars of Independence. At the same time it may be seen that the monte beyond the fence, as well as the river, makes possible for the people of La Laja, most of them from rural backgrounds, a kind of continuity with the life of the country. In their attribution of dangerous supernatural beings to these natural areas they seem to be expressing both their commitment to the man-made world of the barrio, the world of communal life, and the importance which the natural untamed world still has for them.

3.
La Laja as Part of History

Once when I asked a semiskilled worker in San Félix about himself, he began his reply with the words, "I have had a historic life." He went on to explain what he meant by that. He said that he had grown up in a barter economy in the mountainous, rural state of Sucre on the north coast; he had gone to work in the oil camps; now he was an employee of the Orinoco Mining Company in the growing city. He said that even this was not the end of the story: "Industry is the future of the worker," and that industry was what was represented by the steel plant on which he was now an onlooker. I never heard anyone else express this point of view quite so clearly, but my informant's view of his own life as part of history was surely not unique. One of the things which gives life in Ciudad Guayana its particular dynamism is the fact that its participants know themselves to be part of history. If people in the city, if the residents of La Laja often speak, as they do, of "the future," in a general sense aside from their own personal prospects, it is because the world has changed so rapidly in their own lifetimes that they are able to perceive the past as more than a series of events, as representing historical process, continuing into a future.

Life in La Laja, then, has to be understood in part as a segment of history, both because it is so, and because its participants feel it to be so. The processes now going on in La Laja are

part of a set of processes which have been and are now transforming Venezuela from an agricultural country, through a stage of an
economy dominated by extractive enterprise, and into the beginnings of industrialism. The case of La Laja is part of the more
general case of Venezuela. Still more generally, the case of Venezuela is one of a still broader category, the drive of the "backward
nations" to catch up, which is transforming the modern world. We
think of this category in terms of "economic development" because
it is economic transformation which appears to be at the center of
the processes involved, but these processes are, clearly, multiple
and interrelated. It is a trend of history which we also identify
from other points of view with nation-building, with urbanization,
with the spread of literacy and mass communications, with social
mobility, and with changes in social structure.

It was the discovery of oil which propelled Venezuela into this
transformation. Before the end of World War I and the beginnings
of the oil era, Venezuela was a thinly populated country with a
basically agrarian economy. Even in 1936, two-thirds of the population was rural, and 71 percent of Venezuelans were illiterate. The
European and Venezuelan-born elite groups of colonial and independent Venezuela had fused into a small upper-class predominantly white elite. The mixed-bloods and freed Negroes and slaves
of the colonial period had become a highly racially mixed lower
class. (The basic division was class, not race; the elite had a small
admixture of Negro and Indian blood; class lines were very sharply
drawn. Still, the congruence between race and class was sufficiently strong so that even under present conditions of considerable
mobility bridging both race and class the word *negro* (black) may
be used, affectionately as well as derogatingly, as a synonym for
lower class.)

Towns, including the capital, were not large and were dominated by the gentry who were elitist in their point of view and
cosmopolitan in their cultural interests; the children of this class
were often educated in Europe. The elite more or less monopolized
access to education and political and economic power. A survey in
1956 showed 90 percent of all cultivated lands owned by less than
6 percent of the population. Three-quarters of all farmers owned no
land at all, but subsisted as renters, squatters, and agricultural
laborers on the great estates and ranches.

The first large-scale production of petroleum took place in
1917. By 1929 Venezuela was second only to the U.S. in oil produc-

tion, and oil completely dominated the Venezuelan economy. Even at the end of the 1950's, although output in manufacturing had been increasing considerably faster than that in oil, petroleum still accounted for 22 percent of the gross national product, compared to a little over 16 percent for manufacturing. Oil accounted for two-thirds of government revenue and over 90 percent of foreign exchange.

Oil prosperity in Venezuela was a selective prosperity, but it was a glittering enough anomaly to draw thousands of people from the countryside to the oil camps, where construction could employ even totally unskilled workers, and to the cities where a rural migrant might hope to catch some of the economic trickle-down from the first-level recipients of oil riches. The piping in of the new wealth into a social structure with a very narrow apex resulted in a physical concentration of economic opportunity; jobs were in the oil camps and in Caracas, and government money was spent, under the ten-year dictatorship of Pérez Jiménez, predominantly in Caracas in large public works. The most dramatic effect of oil prosperity was a very rapid rate of urbanization. That population which had been still two-thirds rural in 1936 was by 1960 two-thirds urban. The population of Caracas increased by 59 percent during a single decade. By 1950 about 19 percent of native-born Venezuelans were living in a state other than that of their birth; Venezuelans became a people on the move.

Oil prosperity also attracted to Venezuela many immigrants from abroad. Between World War II and 1962, some 683,500 immigrants came to Venezuela—206,800 Spaniards, 188,530 Italians, 55,080 Portuguese. The wave of immigrants concentrated in the large centers. They became a new technical and commercial middle class. The Italians and Spaniards ran the lumber mills, furniture-making shops, the automobile repair shops and organized a good part of retail trade. The Italians built the steel mill. The majority seem to have come with the idea of making their fortunes and going home again rather than settling in Venezuela, and their relationship to the native Venezuelans was colored by this; still, they served the newly urbanizing mass as a source of technical and organizational expertise.

The structure of industrial wages and labor relations in Venezuela took shape in the context of the oil camps. The oil centers were not only foreign-owned enclaves (99 percent of oil investment is still foreign-owned); they were generally in areas outside towns or cities, lacking not only roads, water, electricity, but schools and hospitals. It became established policy for "the companies" to provide a very large amount of basic infrastructure, not only physical facilities such as roads and housing but also schools and medical care. The tendency to concentrate the provision of social services through the companies was supported by the pattern of labor organization which also, naturally, focused on the limited number of large, often foreign-owned companies. A sharply differentiated wage pattern became established in which a small number of oil and mining companies paid relatively high wages. Additional benefits to workers in the substantial companies usually total 84 to 120 percent of the average basic daily wage. (The petroleum industry, with less than 3 percent of the labor force, recently accounted for half of all wages paid.) Most companies give three or four weeks paid vacation, and a sum equal to two months' pay as an alternative option to an otherwise-required sharing of profits with the workers.

The spread of communications and of medical services made possible by oil resulted in cutting nearly in half the death rate between 1940 and 1960. The population of about 7,600,000 shown in the 1961 census was almost half again as much as it had been in 1950. With an annual gain of nearly 4 percent, Venezuela was one of the fastest-growing countries in the world. It also had one of the world's youngest populations; nearly 42 percent were under fourteen, as compared to less than 27 percent in the United States.

The roads, radios, and schools financed by oil meant not only a sharp rise in literacy—illiteracy dropped from 71 per cent in 1936 to an estimated 26 to 28 percent in 1960—but also a general spread of sophistication of several kinds. There was sophistication in self-presentation; I have seen girls in isolated rural settlements to the south of Ciudad Guayana wearing tight slacks and upswept hairdos in completely urban style. There began to develop that sense of social process which makes it possible for a semieducated worker to say "I have had a historic life," or for another woman, totally illiterate and at the economic margins, to tell me that "education is the future of the people." That sort of sophistication represented by participation in politics became widespread. Among a sample of workers interviewed in 1963 in eastern Venezuela 26.6 percent had attended a political meeting within the last six months and 36.6 percent discussed politics; over 8 percent had participated actively in political work. In Ciudad Guayana the rates of political participation were higher still; the same survey found that 17.5 percent of unskilled workers there had actively participated in politics.

It is probably fair to say that it was oil development which brought popular government to Venezuela. It took thirty years; the first coming-to-power of the leftist liberals was broken by a coup d'etat followed by ten years of dictatorship; but by the time of which I write, the nascent, still-struggling democracy was the center of the political scene. There was around me in La Laja a general commitment to democracy as a better way, with widespread doubt as to whether Venezuela was capable of it. During my stay my neighbors voted in the first election Venezuela had ever had, which replaced a duly-elected national government with a successor chosen in the same manner.

Finally, it was no doubt the experience of rapid social and economic change and of a sudden burst of national prosperity which gave Venezuela a dominant atmosphere which might be described as a kind of idealistic optimism phrased in terms of material progress. In the same 1963 survey mentioned above, among a sample of dwellers in "ranchos"—shacks—two-thirds felt that things in Venezuela were getting better. In a basically optimistic population, the people of Ciudad Guayana are particularly so; they have come to seek their fortunes, and they think they may find them. Among unskilled workers interviewed there, 90 percent said that they expected their situation to improve in the next five years. All over Venezuela, and slightly more in Ciudad Guayana than elsewhere, respondents in the survey showed an almost astonishing tendency to perceive society as open, or at least to claim that "any capable person in Venezuela is able to become" practically anything he chooses; among unskilled workers interviewed in Ciudad Guayana, every level was seen as accessible to all by over 90 percent of the respondents.

In this general national history the history of the Guayana region and of Ciudad Guayana has a special place. The history of Ciudad Guayana has a kind of double dynamic. It is part of an old frontier region of rubber boom and gold rush, a history still continuing through the diamond strikes which are still a more-or-less annual event. This area has now become part of the new frontier of economic development.

When a group of the *gente buena* of San Félix met to form a branch of the national Athenaeum which might serve as a focus for their traditional upper-class cultural aspirations, a speaker from the group—a doctor—gave a brief talk on the history of the town. It was a history seen from the point of view of the local elite, and in the context of the Guayana region with which that elite still tends to identify.

He saw the Guayana as a frontier which had experienced a number of local booms in the past. First came the rubber boom, which brought people flocking to the area around Tumeremo. Later, the gold mines opened at El Peru, and El Peru and El Callao became boom towns full of West Indians, miners, and adventurers from all over eastern Venezuela. Now San Félix had become the site of a boom.

San Félix he saw as a place very different from the old regional towns of his youth. The small regional elite, based on cattle and commerce, had settled into a way of life in such towns with great pride of family and literary cultural interests. Upata, said the speaker, had "names," "families," "tradition." "Here," he said, "we are all adventurers."

When he first came to San Félix in the 1940's, he remembered, it was still seven or eight hours by mule to the district capital of Upata, a trip which now takes less than an hour by automobile on the road built by the Iron Mines Company. San Félix then had one small local generating plant which stopped functioning at eleven in the evening. He had often had to deliver babies by putting his automobile in the plaza and directing the headlights into the windows of his clinic. But the town had grown through waves of in-migration. When the dam at Guarico was finished, he claimed, there was a time when thousands of just-unemployed workers were arriving daily, looking for work around San Félix. "When the Caroní (dam) started building, there were fifteen thousand workers here, six thousand working, the rest hoping." "Now," he said, "in Upata, in Guasipati, in Tumeremo, there almost are no men." He did not mean, of course, that these towns had become depopulated in a literal sense; they have not. But the *gente buena* have left them, and their places have been taken by *gente cualquiera* from the countryside. Members of the old elite, their economic base shaken by the opening up of the region, have had to move to Ciudad Guayana, to Ciudad Bolívar, to Caracas, to try to establish themselves in the new order.

The people of Barrio La Laja are also "adventurers" trying to establish themselves in the new order, but they are adventurers of a very different sort than that remnant of an old regional elite which was trying to organize the Athenaeum in San Félix. They are of that just-urbanizing *gente cualquiera*, people who are, at varying rates of speed, moving out of and up from (the two are not identical) a generally rural base which is not far off historically for any of them.

La Laja began in the 1940's with the establishment in the area of the Iron Mines Company of Venezuela, an American-owned subsidiary of Bethlehem Steel. It began as a settlement of wage laborers for "the company," just outside the company fence.

The "first settlers" of La Laja, who claim to have given the barrio its name, still live in the barrio. They are a couple, the man born in Cuiria on the north coast and the wife from El Callao, the gold-mining town farther south in Guayana, who had been living for ten years in San Félix. When the man got a job with the newly developing Iron Mines Company as a construction worker he decided to make a "country house" near the company property in order to raise chickens to sell to the workers. After a year or so the couple moved to La Laja permanently. The second settler, who also still lives in La Laja and who owns one of the principal stores, came directly from agriculture in the state of Anzoátegui to the north.

When these first settlers arrived, there were two families farming on the site. Their farmlands were in a matter of a few years taken up by building sites. The large house sites of the first settlers were in the same way divided by later comers looking for house sites. The oral history of present residents does not record any unpleasantness over this process, although present house sites, even without a legal basis of ownership (residents of La Laja are "squatters" on publicly-owned land) are strongly respected by custom.

Houses of the settlers were built along the road from the Iron Mines property to San Félix, which at that time ran along the low land parallel to the present road. After some years the company made a new road on higher land, the present highway into town, and installed a turnstile in the entrance to their property to stop vehicular traffic. They then moved back their fence and built a road connection for barrio use to the new highway. The barrio is thus a strip development, squeezed sideways into triangular shape by the limitations of terrain.

All of the first wave of settlers were either working for the Iron Mines Company or, as in the case of a Chinese family who for some years ran a bakery in La Laja, selling to the market of Iron Mines workers. As people remember those days, the barrio was much more prosperous than it is now. The company was in the period of exploration and building. Jobs for unskilled men were plentiful. Iron Mines alone is said to have had as many as thirty contractors, with up to 500 men each. There was much commerce in the barrio. Boats stopped every day, buying and selling.

Although many of the early residents came out of a rural background more or less directly, they seem to have quite determinedly set their sights on wage labor. The first settlers' "country house" soon became merely a dwelling house with a small yard, and later comers seem not to have made any serious attempt to combine wage labor with the growing of corn and yucca. The cash economy has always been the focus of La Laja.

During this early period the first residents were not only getting settled in the barrio; they were, in the case of the men, getting used to working for the company. "It was like a school; no one knew how to do the work when they came, but the company would put in someone with experience to show how." In their recollections of this period, the men do not recall any particular difficulty in adjusting to fixed hours of work. The company blew a siren at six, but one had to have a watch at home since it was necessary to leave at twenty minutes to six to be there on time.

During this early period the workers were also learning about unionism. Part of the oral history of La Laja is the history of the four strikes with the Iron Mines Company. Men who participated in these have no difficulty in recalling the strikes and the details of each settlement. The first strike was a "wildcat": "Just the workers talking together." At that time the company paid five bolívares a day. "So one day the workers came but they wouldn't go in. They just stood there, and said they wouldn't work unless the pay was raised. Then Mr. Trumbull, who was the boss then, was all by himself and became frightened that they would attack him physically, so he said, 'All right, seven bolívares everyone.' Everyone was very content." Later strikes were union-organized, the organizers apparently having for the most part learned the relevant skills in the oil camps. The fourth strike was arbitrated by the government which "told the workers to go back to work and it would deal with the company." Like the preceding three, this one also resulted in clear gains for the workers.

In the early days of La Laja, malaria was a terrible problem. "You would hear the church bell ringing and know of another death." "The Company" provided medical care only for workers, not for workers' dependents as now, and medical care in San Félix was inadequate. By the end of the first decade medical care was improving and malaria had been eradicated by DDT spraying. (The feelings of present residents about DDT spraying are mixed, however; it is believed that the spraying kills not only chickens but also cats, giving the rats a free rein.)

La Laja got a school in 1950, and in 1961 the first earth-walled school building was replaced by a modern two-room structure of concrete with glass-louvered windows. In 1952 a water line was installed in the barrio and many families ran water lines into their houses. (There were, as mentioned, three public taps, but the faucets in these soon got broken, leaving the public taps inoperable.) This lasted for more than two years, at which time, because of the need for water in the rapidly growing neighboring barrio of El Roble, the water was cut off, and the community again became dependent on the river and the water trucks. In 1962 the community installed a new water line, connected to nine public taps; this time private tapping of the line was forbidden. In 1960 the town government of San Félix provided La Laja with a small gasoline generator. The head of the Acción Democrática party in the barrio was its custodian. He explains the barrio's success in negotiating for the generator as having been, in part, connected with an attempt on the part of the local government—all Acción Democrática—to get control of La Laja away from the leftists who were strong there at the time, and, it is said, bringing arms in from the Orinoco. This small generator, which provided weak current from six to ten in the evening (except for occasional special arrangement with its manager) was supplanted in 1962 by a regular electric line installed by the national electricity agency on community petition. (This public gain was to some people a private loss, for at the time I left approximately one third of the households in the barrio still had not gathered the economic resources to pay deposit and installation for the new electric system; the old system had, by tacit agreement, served them gratis.) In 1963 the municipal government began to collect La Laja's garbage and trash and transport it to the town dump.

Meanwhile, the rest of the barrio's physical plant was gradually becoming more "urban" and "modern." Sheet aluminum bit by bit replaced thatch for roofs. Starting in the 1950's, cement block began to replace the traditional earth house construction. The 1960's brought a volleyball court and next a baseball diamond.

La Laja is only twenty years old, but in that twenty years is contained a good deal of historical change. The rural-urban migration, the drop in the death rate, the beginnings of industrial employment, the growth of labor unions, the spread of education, the development of democratic politics, the development of urban institutions—all are conspicuous parts of that twenty years of very local history. In the same sense that my informant told me, "I have had a historic life," it could be said that La Laja is a historic neighborhood.

4.
Getting and Spending

Wage labor and the small-scale commerce which is supported by the income from wage labor is the basis of life in La Laja. Production for use is limited and marginal. The world presents itself to the people of La Laja as one which calls for cash to survive and in which over and above bare survival there are very many goods which one would want—to live well—to acquire for cash.

Even if one were to try to reduce one's wants to the minimum, it would be, for all intents and purposes, impossible to produce directly the necessities of life in the barrio. The people of La Laja are still close enough to their rural origins so that about a third of the barrio's families raises animals for food—a pig, or more commonly a few chickens. "*La cria es la vida de los pobres*"—"Raising livestock is the life of the poor"—an unskilled laborer explained to me. But agriculture is marginal enough in the whole Venezuelan economy, and in the city setting, pigs and chickens are a very marginal business indeed. Generally, raising chickens means buying feed. My neighbor, an old lady who was particularly interested in her flock of chickens, was able—although illiterate—to work out the economics of the operation with a high degree of precision and to demonstrate that the cost of fencing was so high as to make her operations break even only if she were to raise at least three flocks successfully. And success in this field is highly problematic; feed is expensive; chickens get sick and die; thefts of roaming poultry are common. Pigs are fed as much as possible from table scraps. But in La Laja it is something of a feat to get enough food on the table for children, let alone for fattening a pig. Thus, the marginal *cria* of La Laja appears more as an expressive activity, and as a way of having a certain meat reserve, than as a major economic resource.

Fruit trees—mangoes, soursops, limes—are common. A couple of families have scrawny patches of corn in the land flooded by the Orinoco during the rainy season. But while one can grow flowers in tin cans filled with soil enriched with rotten wood, one can hardly grow much corn or many vegetables in a place with such limited land area, such poor soil, and lacking rain most of the year.

The natural environment surrounding the barrio is to some extent exploited by its residents. Children collect and eat wild fruits which grow in the brush. Women, especially, collect medicinal plants. Men and boys may catch iguanas and birds to eat, and there is a good deal of fishing in the river. But it is notable that the food resources made available in this way are not only relatively small in amount but rather devalued. Meat—almost all bought and paid for—is greatly preferred to fish, and the river fish are thought of as inferior to the ocean fish brought in by truck from the coast and sold in the market of San Félix. Some residents of La Laja flatly refuse to eat river fish. (My own comparison testing interprets this position as cultural prejudice, rather than as resting on any flavor differential.)

With no need to erect a defense against cold, it would be possible for the people of La Laja to survive with very low-cost housing and clothing. But housing and clothing would in any case cost something. Even if one were to make one's own clothing (and little clothing is in fact made at home) the cloth would have to be bought, and yard goods are expensive in Venezuela. In La Laja, even to build a rural-style mud-walled house one must buy poles, framing, and roofing.

But the people of La Laja do not, by and large, try to get by with the minimum. They are part of that people formed by the oil experience which brought the people of Venezuela new wants and aspirations and spread these new wants and aspirations wide and deep down through the social system.

The standard of dress, for example, is not low. All adults wear shoes, and children generally do. While men in La Laja do not usually own the dark, formal suits of the Venezuelan urban middle class, the khakis which they wear for work and everyday are clean and without patches. Women are greatly interested in style in their clothing. The presentation aspect of women's dress is so strong that even for work around the house they do not cover their dresses with aprons; they will merely wear an older dress for messy work like laundering in the river. When the people of another riverside barrio like La Laja were flooded out and were given clothing by a charitable ladies' organization, they complained to me resentfully that the clothing was secondhand.

As the rural-style *bahareque* houses of which La Laja was once exclusively composed are replaced by houses of cement block, plastered and painted, as sheet aluminum replaces thatch, housing also comes to require sizable cash outlays.

There is, in La Laja, a good deal of buying of upholstered furniture on the installment plan. My family was one of the very few in the barrio which slept only in the hammocks traditional in rural Venezuela. Over half the households have radios. Several families have rather elaborate record players. People buy enamel-ware and plastic dishes, pictures, ornamental shelves. Masculine social life is lubricated by the drinking of beer. People rarely walk any great distance; they take the bus or one of the jitney cabs which charge by the place. To send children to school means school uniforms, new shoes, bus fares, books, and notebooks. There are plenty of things on which to spend money.

Neither goods nor services are typically distributed outside the money economy, except as they move within families. A nurse who knows how to give injections will help anyone in the barrio with her services and not charge. A group of men may join together to donate their labor in building some community facility like a water line, or in cleaning the streets. But these are exceptions.

The first settlers of the barrio say that in their rural homes they were accustomed to the rural customs of housebuilding, in which labor is not hired but in which relatives and neighbors cooperate in building houses. But that, they say, is a custom "of the country," and when people moved to La Laja they did not exchange labor in housebuilding. Either the house owner was working for the company, in which case he had a relatively high income and relatively little time and hired someone to work on his house, or he did it himself "little by little." While a family—including the women—may still work together to put up a *bahareque* house, the house of cement block is generally erected by a hired mason, with whatever collaboration the owner may lend. I noted that some people had engaged relatives to lay blocks for them and were paying these relatives a standard wage.

Reports differ on the question as to whether the rural customs of exchange of food persisted at all when La Laja was new. One informant says that she remembers that "in the old days" when one family butchered a pig they never sold the meat, at least within the barrio, but gave it away to relatives and neighbors—who would, of course, reciprocate when they themselves butchered. Others say that they cannot remember this taking place. It is certain that anyone who now butchers in the barrio will sell the meat, even to his close neighbors.

The economy of La Laja is, then, a cash economy. It is an economy which presents a wide range of consumer goods, which generates wants for the things which take money to buy.

But the burst of economic development which brought the people of La Laja to the new city, and which dangled these wants before them, has so far been imperfectly successful in diffusing through the society the means for satisfying the wants it generated. The Venezuelan- economy came to be a notably uneven one. It came to have a few industries—oil and mining—with high wage scales, a range of other economic activities providing comparatively low incomes, and a high level of unemployment. The national census in 1961 showed seventeen out of every hundred nonagricultural workers out of a job.

The city of which La Laja is a part is a new, still building, industrial city in the interior; it is not an ordinary, typical city. But its economic structure is Venezuelan development summarized. The economic base of Ciudad Guayana consists of three relatively high-wage companies, including the government-owned steel plant. The wages paid by "the companies" support the people of the city, either directly or as the basis of the city's commercial life. But this superstructure of commerce and services, although conspicuous, is still relatively undeveloped. In 1961, commerce—almost all retail— occupied only a tenth of the economically active population, as compared to 18 percent nationally. Of the city's labor force 16 percent was in services, compared to 35 percent in the nation.

A study made by the Venezuelan Central Bank in 1962 showed the distribution of incomes in the new city also characteristically Venezuelan in its unevenness. A fourth of the *employed* persons in Ciudad Guayana were getting less than 7 percent of the wages and salaries paid there, while the 5 percent with the highest incomes got about 18 percent of the total. Among families with at least one wage earner, 37 percent had incomes of less than 500 bolívares—about $111 a month. Meanwhile, nearly a quarter of the economically active population was unemployed.

As for Barrio La Laja itself, in the fall of 1962 when I censused its inhabitants, I found that of its 490 residents, living in eighty household groups, there were only eighty-one persons employed. This was partly because the barrio had so many children and young people that fully work-age adults (aged nineteen to fifty) were only 34 percent of the population. And of these, many were unemployed. Of the grown males between nineteen and sixty years of age, over a third reported themselves unemployed, with the rate of unemployment highest (about 40 percent) among the young men of nineteen to thirty and those in their fifties. Thus, the eighty-one persons in the barrio with regular earnings were supporting, on an average, five others—children or unemployed adults. Regular earnings, ranging down to 150 bolívares a month (for some domestic workers), were having to be spread, in many cases, rather thin.

Of the employed persons in La Laja, the largest group (twenty-one persons) worked at the steel mill. Eleven were employed by the Orinoco Mining Company, the U.S. Steel subsidiary across the Caroní River. Seven worked for the nearby Iron Mines Company, which had been the first impetus for the settlement. Eleven were in commerce, either as owners of small grocery and refreshment businesses or as ambulant salesmen. Twelve women were domestic servants or washed and ironed, almost all of them in one or the other of the two company "camps." Nineteen persons had various jobs from school teacher to cab driver.

Much of the commercial activity took place in La Laja itself. The barrio had at the time of my census six "businesses"—roughly one for every eighty-one inhabitants or for every twelve households. One was a small construction-board stand, selling bananas and groceries, owned by a family living in a small earth-daub house in the most physically and socially marginal part of the barrio, but the proprietor was one of the four car owners in La Laja at the time, having bought a second-hand vehicle to use in hauling goods. Four businesses were more substantial *abastos* selling in tiny quantities such staples as bread, plantains, sugar, margarine, powdered milk, soft drinks, and beer, and serving as social centers where men might sit and play dominoes, drink beer, or, in one case, play pool on a couple of battered pool tables. The latter *abasto* had almost gone out of the grocery business, being perpetually out of stock, and was in effect a small pool hall. The sixth business was a licensed "bar," with dancing to the jukebox in the evenings, especially on weekends. The barrio had had for some weeks a seventh business, a small one-freezer meat market, but this had proved too weak to survive even in the very small-bore commercial world of La Laja; the quantity of meat eaten in La Laja is not great, and people preferred to carry their supply from the market or the company commissaries, where the quality was better and the price lower. All owners of these businesses were residents of the barrio.

Still later I was able to watch from my front door the evolution of another local business. A kinsman of the woman who ran the bar, a middle-aged man with some experience in masonry, but then unemployed, erected a tiny board stand at the end of the street, at which he sold cigarettes and snacks, but which served also as the locus of a tiny gambling hall—four bingo cards laid out on a bench. Bingo being popular, but not of a scale to support even a single man of moderate needs, he and his kinswoman of the bar shortly evolved an expansion of the bingo idea; Juan would build a cockfighting pit next to the bar, where he would stage cockfights to which he would charge admission and where he could fight his own cocks. Neither believed that even this enlarged appeal to the gambling instinct would turn up any considerable profit, but they considered that the custom drawn to the bar and its beer trade—by which Juan was then, after all, being supported too—would more than make up for even a minor loss on the cocks. The scheme seemed to me plausible enough, although when I left it was still to be tested; Juan had built the cockpit and succeeded after prolonged negotiation in getting a municipal permit to hold cockfights, but he was still dickering for the police surveillance legally required at these occasions.

None of the businessmen of La Laja keeps accounts; none of them, I believe, is capable of doing so. None of them was able to tell me with any precision what the sales were. This does not necessarily mean, however, that they do not understand the general outlines of their economic situation. The owner of the bar, for example, was able to run over her expenses—for the license, for the jukebox rental, for electric current to run the jukebox and the two refrigerators—and to calculate that she would be running a profitable enterprise only if she could greatly increase her custom—either through the cockfight expedient or by somehow financing purchase of a chicken-broiler which would, by making food available, discourage the drinkers from leaving to eat. In the meantime, she was, in effect, subsidizing the expansion of the bar out of her husband's salary as an electrician with "the company."

The bar is the most impressive business in La Laja. None of La Laja's businesses is of a volume to be "really" profitable; they continue in terms of a situation in which the opportunity cost to the entrepreneur is, in effect, zero. Meanwhile, observations would suggest that they are perpetuated not only by the tiny incomes they supply but as much or more by a sort of return not easily entered on a bookkeeper's balance sheet: the pleasure of social interaction and the self-esteem which comes from having a visible capital and from exercising the skills of entrepreneurship.

The wages from "the companies" support commercial life not only by becoming the money which, paid over the counter, is the receipts in the till, but generally by being the source of the capital which makes it possible to found businesses. Those whose earnings from wage labor are more than enough to cover family expenses (and size of family may be the crucial variable here—it is hardly chance that one of the most well-kept houses and handsomest garden in the barrio belong to a bachelor) not infrequently try to invest in some return-bringing capital equipment. On a small scale this may mean buying a refrigerator, which besides serving the family's food-storage needs makes possible a tiny business in ice and Pepsi-Cola. To start a tiny grocery takes very little more. Another common way of translating money capital into a source of income is to build or buy a house for rental. About a dozen persons living in the barrio own houses in the barrio which they rent to others. Some persons have houses in San Félix or El Roble, renting for up to 400 bolívares a month. At the time of my census three houses were being built in the barrio specifically for rental.

"The companies" are important in capital-formation at the individual level not only as a source of capital, but as agglomerators of capital; it is those lump-sum payments made annually under Venezuelan labor law, or, on a larger scale, the substantial payments to employees on termination of employment, which characteristically get translated into refrigerators and rental houses. My informant and friend Señor Figueres recognized this when he told me that companies should retain their employees long enough so that each employee, when finally laid off, would have enough capital to set himself up in some business for the rest of his life. If they keep hiring and laying people off, he said, the people are just back in the street again, because their termination pay is small and will just be drunk up.

This observation—correct enough, accepting its premise—suggests another function for that barrio commerce, so irrational in narrow economic terms. In the personalist, egalitarian world of the barrio, it is hard to turn down the comradely conviviality of the bar. Thus it is very hard to save out of regular income. A business, or a house under construction, serves also as a way of legitimizing and enforcing saving.

"The companies," then, in a number of ways set the pattern of economic possibilities for the people of La Laja, but their jobs do not constitute the entire field of possibilities; during my stay, people of La Laja worked at school teaching, cab driving, nursing at the hospital, door to door selling, social work with the development agency, and one returned to rural farming, south of the city.

The growth of "the companies" created La Laja, which is basically a settlement of people economically attached to "the companies," either through direct employment, or indirectly—as by cab driving, domestic service—or, in the case of unemployed persons, in hope of some connection. Some men who were employed by the companies early were able to capitalize that employment into technical skill which gave them a relatively secure footing in the company system or into a working capital which—in the form of a tiny business, or a rental house—at least gave them some income security when "the company gave them their time." Others passed in and out of the company employment without establishing such a niche in the system. When the companies were in the stage of construction and there were plenty of unskilled jobs to be had, they worked; when the construction was done and production processes called for fewer people of more skill, they lost their footing. Now they work intermittently at one thing and another and spend a good deal of their more-than-ample free time in the bar.

There is a pattern of economic development often spoken of as the "dual economy," characteristic of areas which, even after undergoing considerable economic development in certain sectors, perpetuate ways of life in which traditional economic practices are embedded in traditional social forms and cultural practices. In such economies, one segment of the population participates in the modern economy of cash exchanges, mass produced goods, and wage labor; another segment still lives in a traditional world based on subsistence production with only limited participation in the mass market cash economy. A part of the society may be said to be industrialized or urbanized, the world of the "moderns," and alongside this sector continues the traditional world of the "peasants."

When one thinks of those families who live on the outskirts of Ciudad Guayana with their chickens and corn patches, who say *"La cria es la vida de los pobres,"* who share the buses with hard-hatted steel workers as they come to town for occasional shopping and occasional wage labor, the phrase "dual economy" seems to sum up the situation aptly. But the situation in La Laja is less adequately summarized in this way. La Laja has definitely thrown in its lot with the city and the cash economy. *"Los pobres"* in La Laja may raise a few chickens, but they cannot really make a living that way. They are, in fact, making a living on the others, on the persons in the barrio who have found themselves niches in the modern sector of the economy. Their cognitive orientation is toward the modern world of mass-produced consumption goods, and toward the world of personal relations giving them access to it. Because they do not have the skills, they cannot be full participants in that world, but they are hangers-on.

The situation here seems to be less aptly termed a "dual economy" than an economy which is "bipolar." In such a society as that of Venezuela and of Ciudad Guayana, no less than of New York City, everyone from top to bottom is, in effect, committed to the same cash economy. The difference between those at the top and those at the bottom is not so much in the sector to which they direct their efforts as it is in their greatly varying ability to cope with and participate in it. At the top of the system a group of people with technical and managerial skills are able to use the opportunities provided by economic development in order to live well, consuming the goods provided by the economy and training their children in the skills needed to continue this style of life. At the bottom is a large pool of unemployed or under-employed people who would like to imitate, superficially at least, the style of life of those at the upper levels but who do not have the skills to do so nor are organized so as to provide their children with those skills.

The economic life of La Laja is a part of such a bipolar economy.

The social world of Barrio La Laja is not that of an isolated village or small community in which everyone knows everyone else. People are always moving in and out; nearly a quarter of the barrio's adults had been there less than a year; and at no time does each person there know all the others personally, or by name. There is no single institution or group of institutions in the barrio to which all residents belong. Moreover, everyone in the barrio has connections—economic, kinship, social—outside the barrio. Each person's field of social relations includes part, but not all, of the barrio, the proportion varying greatly according to age, length of residence, economic role, and number of kin. At the same time each person's field of social relations spreads outside the barrio as well, some to a much greater extent than others.

The social world of the barrio is in some ways typically urban in form. It is perhaps even more striking, therefore, that relations based on kinship or assimilated to kinship are dominant in the social network. People are likely to have relatives living nearby. In this barrio, to which nearly half the adults have migrated within the last five years, two-thirds of the households are connected by kinship with at least one other household in the barrio. People, especially women, interact with their kin. People aid their kinsfolk economically. Kinship terms are used in address much more generally than they are in the United States at any social level. One greets a kinsman as "cousin" or some other appropriate term rather than by name.

The kinship model is extended to other relationships. It seems natural to treat a person, especially a younger person, with whom one is on any basis of intimacy, as though he or she were a kinsman. A neighbor's child may be addressed as "son" or "daughter;" two little girls who play together habitually come to address each other as "sister."

Moreover, to these biological kin are added one's *compadres* and *comadres,* a group of chosen kinsfolk. For each child, a parent will choose three pairs of godparents, one for the little baptismal ceremony performed in the house by laymen, one for the formal church baptism usually held when the child is three years old or so, and one for the first communion. The godparents have certain obligations to the godchild, most notably in the case of the first communion godparents, the buying of the elaborate costume which is de rigueur on this occasion; but, although the Church defines the godparent-godchild relationship as primary in the situation, La Laja places in practice most stress on the relationship established through *compadrazgo* between the child's own parents and his ritual parents. The importance placed on the relationship is symbolized in the way they always address each other, not by name but as *compadre* or *comadre.*

Since it has often been thought and said that kinship relations tend to become less important in the urban setting, this situation might be thought of as anomalous, an evidence of a transition still incomplete from rural to urban life. But there may be more to it than that. Among the working-class population of Panama City and of Mexico City, among Puerto Rican migrants to New York, kinship relations seem to be at least as important and perhaps more important than among their rural counterparts. The work of such social researchers as Michael Young has exposed strong kinship networks in segments of British urban society. But in addition, a look at the nature of the kinship networks in such urban areas suggests that they may in fact be shaped by the necessities of urban life: that they are a folkish plant which springs up from the very city pavements.

In taking a look at kinship in La Laja, the primary unit used will be the household. "The family" seems hardly to exist as a social unit with discrete boundaries; certainly in La Laja there is nothing comparable to those kinship groups functioning as corporate entities which are reported for some African societies. Kinship ties are extended bilaterally; husband and wife each continue to have their own kinship networks. People may speak of "the Rodrigues" as of a social unit, but such a naming seems to designate a sort of conspicuous clot of kinship relations, connecting with other such clots rather than a distinct group for which one can easily enumerate members and nonmembers. The household, on the other hand, is a unit rather clearly defined at any point of time by the units of physical cohabitation, except for a few marginal cases in which a single aged parent is living in a separate house next door to grown children and may be considered as forming for some purposes part of a single household with them. It is not, of course, a unit with long-term boundaries; since people join not only by birth but also by affiliation for social and economic reasons, or, on the other hand, move out to join other households or to establish households of their own. Nor is the kinship structure fully described by an enumeration of households, for the households are, as already noted, more generally than not connected to others by kinship. The grouping called in the barrio "the Campos" (that is, the Campos "family") includes the personnel of four households, totaling thirty-six persons more or less, in which the maternal generation consists of six sisters; two other households are related to this core.

But as a point from which to begin, the household is a convenient unit. An analysis was made of the composition of La Laja's eighty households, and this was supplemented by interviewing on values and practices with regard to family and household organization in an attempt to analyze the principles which seem to govern household structuring. The following "principles" attempt to describe how families are actually structured in terms of the cultural and social factors which seem involved in giving them their characteristic form.

1) Normally, a household consists of persons related to each other by blood or marriage.

Of the eighty households of La Laja, six violate this rule. Four of the cases involve the taking-in of older unmarried persons with no kin living nearby: two old men, unrelated, live together; two other households consist of small nuclei of related single men and another bachelor friend; in one household an extremely poor old woman living with her grandchild has taken in an even poorer beggar woman. One family has an adoptive child of no blood relationship to them (adoption of kinship-related children is not rare). In the sixth case, an older male house-owner had been sharing his house for a month with a young couple, unrelated to him, with their two children. In all other cases, the people living in a single household were in some way related by kinship.

2) The primary axis of kinship structure is the relationship between a mother and her children, her own or adoptive.

Men, it is felt, ought to support and care for their children but women "have to" care for their children. The children have a reciprocal obligation, not quite so strong, to care for their mother. Although both these reciprocal obligations seem to imply both an element of practical aid and one of sentiment, the parent-child relationship seems to be more weighted on the side of practical care and support, that of child to parent more on the side of sentiment. Poetry about mothers is especially read by and at times composed by more educated persons; however, a group of *clase obrero* teenagers in publishing a weekly newspaper also inserted a number of examples of literature on this theme. When my husband was killed in an automobile accident while I was living in the barrio, two people commented that one must be able to adjust to anything; "one can *even* adjust to the death of one's mother."

Women may have and rear children without a husband. If a young woman has children while living in her parents' home and later marries a man other than the father of her first children, she will ordinarily bring the children with her to the marriage. (There are some exceptions to this, in which the tie between mother and child has been extended and transferred to the mother's mother; adoption by the mother's sister also seems not uncommon.) When marriages break up, as they not rarely do, the children always stay with the mother. Usually, the women and children also retain the house. Thus, in the working-class household the woman is typically the effective head of the household, even if

3) the man, when and if present, is formally the *jefe familia* or "head of the family." He should be treated with respect by both wife and children. He may strike his wife as well as his children. However, conspicuous wife-beating is not common, and women can and do leave men who drink or mistreat them. One of the few cases of real violence in La Laja during the time I was living there was when a grown daughter cracked her father's head open when he tried to beat her mother.

4) Ordinarily, a couple with an established marital relationship, whether legalized or common-law union, should establish a household of their own. This applies with especial force to the combination of parents and married children.

Only four households in La Laja contain more than one married pair. In one, the principal nuclear family has added to it the man's first cousin with his wife and children. In another, the husband's sister and her husband share the household with the principal pair; the "extra couple" have no children. The third is a case in which the wife's brother, with his wife and children, shares the house. In only one case are the two married pairs of successive generations. Here a grown daughter's common-law husband (he has legally recognized her child) lives in the household with his wife, his wife's parents, and his wife's siblings. This situation has been of short duration and seems unstable; it appears that it will be resolved either by the younger couple getting their own house or by their relationship breaking up. There are plenty of three-generation households in La Laja, but with the exception cited, either the first or second generation or both is a *mujer sola*—a woman without husband either in law or common law.

The standard pattern on marriage, either legal and formal, or through informal custom or elopement, is one of neolocal residence; the man usually locates a place to live and the woman joins him there. It is felt that women are jealous of their sons' wives for taking away the son's support from themselves (a belief clearly related to principle 2, the primacy of the mother-child relationship). It is supposedly easier to have the man join his wife's family than the other way around, but even here the young husband is in a peripheral position (due to the close mother-daughter tie), and if there is a father-in-law in the house, he finds the situation difficult to reconcile with ideas of *machismo* and formal masculine dominance (principle 3).

Since living with the parental generation is not a valid alternative, as it is the preferred one in some societies, it follows that something of a solid economic base is essential to a marriage; the couple has to pay a separate rent. It would appear that some stable relationships evolving toward marriage break up before they even get started, so to speak, in the practical and economic difficulties of establishing a separate household. The man then drifts away, and the girl is left, perhaps with a child or two, living in her parents' house.

5)There is considerable separation between the world of men and of women. In the evenings a man is likely to be drinking beer with his male friends, while his wife visits with her women friends on her front doorstep or on theirs. The world of men is more *en la calle*—the world of the bars, movie theaters, etc.; women are more likely to stay close to home.

6) Siblings in general have egalitarian and mutually supporting relationships. The tie between sisters is likely to be especially strong, perhaps because of the greater common focus on the home.

7) Marriage is conceived of as an alliance between individuals rather than family groups.

In a "proper" marriage, the young man asks the parents of his intended spouse for their permission, but this custom seems often honored in the breach, and there seems to be none of the reciprocal exchange of calls and gifts which in some Latin American societies makes marriage establish relationships between the family groups of the two married persons. It seems to be possible for a marriage to survive the active hostility of the parental generation, for the mother of one young woman in the barrio still does not speak to her daughter's (legally married) husband after five years and two children. This attitude does not seem to cause any serious problems, for the mother regards her daughter's marriage, while a mistake, as her business; and the husband puts no obstacles in the way of his wife's considerable visiting and economic aid to the mother. The married couple and the mother live at about ten houses' distance from each other.

It is not uncommon for marriage to take place by having the girl "go off" with the man; this may be followed by legal marriage, or it may not. Church marriage is of distinctly higher social prestige than a merely legal marriage, and the latter higher than common-law residence, but aside from this status gradient there seem few social sanctions on failure to legalize. Church marriages are uncommon in La Laja. People say that they are expensive, by which they presumably mean not so much the ceremony itself as the outlay in dress and festivities which the status implications of a church wedding bring to it. Women in La Laja also comment that a church marriage is bad because it permits no divorce. It is a contract with no escape clause in a society where separation often seems appropriate.

It may be seen that there is a general correlation between the status implications of the marriage form, the formality in legal and ritual terms of the marriage, and the degree of masculine dominance implied. At one extreme is the middle-class-style legalized marriage with the husband clearly the *jefe familia*, the house and property generally his, and the husband's economic and social role highly status-defining for his wife and children. At the other is the

definitely matrifocal family of the working class, organized around
a woman and her children; the house (probably the only substantial property) is the woman's, and "husbands" attach themselves
peripherally for longer or shorter periods, and with greater or
smaller degrees of definiteness. This structure is perfectly acceptable socially in La Laja, but it is clearly seen as of lower social status
than the first. The status gradient here suggested seems clearly
implied by other behavior; for example, there appears to be a
distinct tendency for those who get married in church to practice
other behavior characteristic of the middle class, such as keeping
their children particularly clean and well dressed.

Marriages, especially common-law ones of the matrifocal type,
may be, and are, terminated by either party. "He left me for
another woman." "He drank much and I decided to spend the rest
of my years in peace with my children." A woman unhappy with
her husband may hang on until her children are somewhat grown
and then take advantage of the solidarity of mother and children to
rely on their mutual support.

A woman with no man in the house is at an economic disadvantage, since there are relatively few jobs for women at the *obrero*
level and those which exist tend to be poorly paid. There is petty
business, especially buying and selling of snacks, a highly marginal
sort of economic enterprise. There is domestic service, but unless
one is able to get a steady job with one of the relatively few
well-to-do families in town—one of the Americans in the "American
camp" will be the best-paying possibility—this is likely to mean
occasional washing and ironing. There is also prostitution, but this
also seems to be a marginal and occasional affair except for women
who operate as regular professionals in one or another of the
houses. I know of no case of this sort in La Laja, although a
prostitute I know from another barrio did find it possible to combine regular nightly work at a "house" with keeping a houseful of
children going in another part of town. But the point must be made
here that for many women in La Laja, having a man in the house is
no firm solution of the economic problem either, because the man is
likely to be unskilled, to be employed only intermittently, and to
be expensive to keep in food and beer when out of work. The man
or men with whom a woman forms connections are, then, from the
economic point of view, just a series of additional possibilities in a
life which consists of a continual scramble to make ends meet and
a juggling of resources to get the children fed on any given day.

The social workers of the Corporación de Guayana, like other well-to-do Venezuelans, deplore the "weakness of family structure" among the poor, as represented by the instability of conjugal relationships and the very high national rate of legal illegitimacy. While I was living in La Laja, the Corporación social workers conducted classes in family life in San Félix intended to promote more stable nuclear families. Their treatment of the problem as basically one of cultural practices, to be changed by education and alteration of convictions, might be compared to the way in which the rather similar patterns in American Negro families have been interpreted as an aspect of handed-down cultural practices—either a reinterpretation of the African matriarchal family or derived from practices developed under conditions of slavery. A more structural point of view seems more plausible to me. Like those writers who relate the prevalence of female-headed families among American Negroes to the social and economic conditions which fail to support the role of the male in the family situation, I was inclined to see the persistence of marriages as the thing to be explained, and to find supporting factors lacking in the conditions of life in La Laja.

In some societies, family groups are important economic units; this is particularly true in peasant agricultural societies, where it is the family that runs the farm which is the basis of life. In La Laja, there is no need for the family to stick together to manage property; property, besides personal clothing and effects, consists at best of ownership of a house and furniture, perhaps crucial to a woman with children to care for but not to the husband. There is no necessary economic collaboration through sex division of labor, for men can in a pinch cook or eat out and women can in a pinch earn a living. Compare the Eskimo, where a man with no woman to sew furs and prepare food for him is in almost as serious a plight as the woman with no man to hunt for her. In La Laja, husband and wife move in distinct worlds—neither requires the other. In the absence of corporate kin groups, marriage cannot be used to cement a useful alliance between families; there is no process analogous to the transfer of the marriage cattle which in African tribal society mobilizes the kin groups to pressure husband and wife to maintain a difficult relationship. In La Laja the bilateral extension of kinship ties is likely to be a dispersive factor, if anything, as kinsfolk of husband and wife make their claims for aid which conflict with the claims of the nuclear family. In many societies, ranging from some Mexican Indian villages to the American young-corporation-executive suburb, there is a game of status which is played in couples; it is the husband and wife together who do the things which move one up through the system. For the working-class world of La Laja, in which people are scrambling to "defend themselves," as people put it, such considerations do not apply.

There remain as functions for the family sexual gratification, the procreation of children, and the rearing of the young. The first two clearly require the collaboration of a couple, but there is no necessity for the same couple to remain together over time to serve these two functions. Often they do not. Both men and women are active and individualistic in sex, quick to form new alliances. For rearing children, continuity is required, but this function may be served in La Laja as in Harlem by the consanguine family organized around mother and children.

It seemed to me, therefore, that the "matrifocal family" arises naturally out of the conditions of lower-class life, whether in Venezuela or elsewhere, especially under conditions of high unemployment; the steady job is seen as relevant in providing men with status and roles which might become the foci for stabilizing the conjugal relationship.

Thus, it is not remarkable that marriages in La Laja are not likely to be particularly stable or permanent. It is more remarkable that about half the households of La Laja consist of more or less stable nuclear family groups—a married (legally or in custom) pair and their children—with or without the addition of other kinsfolk.

The situation with respect to marriage just described does result, not infrequently, in the creation of household groups with a female head. Even excluding single women living alone (in all cases elderly, usually living near their grown children), about a fifth of the households in La Laja were headed by women. The economic position of these households is, as noted, likely to be difficult, unless the woman has a grown son who is employed. If not, the household will usually be supported by domestic service work—for example, laundering—for which wages are low. Two large households in La Laja of eleven and twelve persons had no grown males and no claimed income at all; they were evidently surviving on help from kin and occasional earnings in domestic work, and perhaps occasional prostitution. Both of these households were ones in which sisters were living together with their children.

The tendency to focus on the tie between mother and children results in a number of household groups in La Laja which are in effect small matrilineal lineages of three generations: a woman and her daughters and their children. The only four-generation household in a barrio with very few old people is such a matrilineal lineage. It consists of a man and woman with their five children, the wife's mother and brother, and the husband and two children of the eldest daughter. This family owns and operates a small shop. The shop is referred to in the barrio as the "house of Victoria" rather than identified with reference to the male who is formally the "family head." Another three-generational lineage household of eleven persons has five children in the youngest generation, the children of two of the daughters, in one case involving one father and in the other two; none of the "husbands" in any of the three generations are present in the household.

There appears to be a tendency for lack of economic resources in money or skills to be associated with a certain kind of kinship structure which tends to perpetuate the lack of money and skills in the next generation. Families at this bottom level do not experience the social or economic pressures which would hold together the relationship between husband and wife: therefore, this relationship tends to be weak and to sever altogether. There is a good likelihood that the children of the unskilled will grow up in families in which, lacking an adult male wage earner, the general economic disabilities are multiplied. Such children are likely to be poorly fed and clothed; they are likely to attend elementary school irregularly and to stop school early. Such families not only fail to provide models of successful economic and social achievement, they lack a clear masculine model altogether. That a general outcome of cumulative nonsuccess is not inevitable is shown by one family of mother and sons in La Laja in which the sons seem to be developing as notably successful achievers. But the likelihood that lack of success in one generation will be multiplied in the next seems clear.

It seems possible to look at the relationship between kinship structure and economic situation even more generally. If the family is not an economic unit, and partly for this reason may hardly be said to exist as "a unit" at all, what is the reason for the family ties which link the majority of La Laja's households together? Why do the people of La Laja, moving about in the labor market as so many individual labor units, still form a network of social ties largely defined by kinship? If *the* family is not crucial, why are familial relationships so important?

Let us start from a summary of the nature of these relationships. The social structure of La Laja may be described most generally as a series of partly overlapping networks of highly personalized kinship relations and of personal relations often made into quasi-kinship through *compadrazgo*. Kinship relations are developed bilaterally. There is a good deal of choice in the kinship ties to be stressed; beyond the tie between mother and children, defined around the physical dependence of the young child, it is open to a given individual to select, in large part, which of the many possible kinship relations he is to develop into strong ties. This selection then is made with regard to considerations of the pleasures and advantages, including conomic advantages, of a particular association compared to others. This element of individual choice, taken together with the bilaterality of the system, reduces the tendency of the kinship system to produce distinct corporate groups and exaggerates the tendency of the system to produce networks of relationship. Then, to the real kinsfolk are added additional ties and relationships of chosen, fictitious kinsfolk through the *compcdre* system.

It must be recalled again that kinship networks of similar form are reported for groups similarly placed in the economic order in places as diverse culturally as Mexico City and New York. The basis of these networks of kinship and kinship-like relations seems to lie in the very structure of the economic situation which makes for that sort of matrifocal family structure often looked at by the middle class observer as "weak" or lacking in form. In the urban setting the kinship and quasi-kinship network is a basis of economic security—perhaps not a solid basis, but the basis that is available.

People who work at unskilled labor in an economy to which they are necessarily marginal as individuals, and which has a continuing high rate of unemployment, can rarely accumulate capital. When they are working their continuance at work is unsure, and they are often out of a job. Out of a paying job, there is little they can do to make a living; one cannot in such a setting live off the land or by farming. There is, for the people of La Laja, no organized public welfare system to which to turn. If you are desperate the town council might tide you over with a small gift. With luck you might get on the list to receive occasional packages of American surplus food. But there is no "welfare" in the American sense.

A person's kinsmen, then, are the people to whom one can turn for support. A young man who is out of a job will find a brother, an aunt, a cousin who will house and feed him while he looks for work to turn up. A household with no current income being brought in by any of its members directly will draw on other related households of kin who do have some access to cash. Thus, the two sisters who lived next door to me with their children survived for months on what might have been censused as "no income"; the children were neither healthy nor well-dressed, but they did not starve. At times one or the other of the two women would have work doing washing or ironing. The rest of the time they were "helped" by the grown daughter of one of them who worked as a cleaning woman for me, and who, since her husband worked intermittently, was able to detach some of her earnings for her mother, and by another sister who lived in the house behind them and whose husband, a ship's cook, would have had a good income if he had not drunk so much of it. In La Laja, with one out of three adult males out of a job, and nearly half the population under thirteen, only one person out of six had any regular income. The other five-sixths were apparently living—if precariously—off the employed segment. It was the social networks in which kinship relations are basic which made this possible.

The sort of kinship structure seen in La Laja, then, seems to operate as a system of social and economic welfare in an environment otherwise uncertain in the extreme. Its very looseness makes it possible for any given individual to maximize his possibilities for eliciting help. He will join the household kin group at a particular time most able to take care of him; he will make the kinship claim to the relative who at the time he needs help is most likely to be able to give him help. This welfare function of the kinship network in turn serves to draw kinsfolk into physical proximity; because claims are made in quite personalized terms it is hard to assert a claim in the absence of personal contact and a personally developed relationship.

The looseness and personalization of the kinship structure makes possible a large degree of social differentiation and social mobility without breaking kinship relationships. The more socially or economically successful individual is not devalued because he is seen to interact with unsuccessful kinsfolk. He is not seen as a member of a kin *group,* but as an individual, with ties, based on kinship, to other individuals. A particularly interesting example of this principle was the party which was given by a nurse in the barrio, an intelligent woman highly oriented toward mobility goals. The party was given in the (not highly presentable) house and shop which she shared with her husband, an extremely likable but illiterate man who lacked any middle-class manners. Also in evidence were the woman's parents, both illiterate laborers. The guests were largely semiprofessionals (a beauty parlor operator, schoolteachers, anesthetists, and other minor professional staff from the hospital), and their automobiles completely filled the little street in front of the house.

At the same time, the sort of kinship structure seen in La Laja does put a strain on mobility in the continual draining-off of resources from the successful individual. There is an evident conflict between the middle-class focusing of resources on the educational and other mobility needs of the nuclear family and the working-class pattern of dispersal of resources to needy kin. The situation suggests one prevailing in some American Indian tribes which developed social systems in some ways similar as a response to the uncertainties of a hunting and gathering economy, and where the individual is, in effect, presented with a choice between being a nice fellow, sharing his windfalls with others, or being a bastard and getting ahead.

If the successful people in La Laja were to be captured by doctrines of mobility success, were to save their money and to educate their young, what would become of everyone else? How would the welfare load—that other five-sixths of the population—be taken care of? Even if the larger society were to develop the impersonal welfare institutions to keep them fed and clothed, would it not materially alter their situation? Is there not a difference between being someone's cousin at the moment out of a job, and being a welfare client?

It should be noted, in addition, that the looseness and personalism of the kinship network—added to the practical difficulties of communicating without telephones, where bus fare is an appreciable budget item, and where people find it hard to express themselves in writing—make kinship ties very vulnerable to distance. An old woman in La Laja who has a daughter living about three miles away in Dalla Costa finds that she gets very little help from her daughter and talks of trying to find a house near her daughter. The haphazard growth of the city has made it not too difficult for kinsfolk to settle near each other. But a planned neighborhood means a greater degree of economic segregation, and generally a tighter organization which tends to make this more difficult. As the city grows it will be harder for poor relatives to live near their more successful kin except by actually moving in with them.

All of these factors suggest a gradual layering-off of the present *clase obrero*, as it now appears in La Laja, into two groups. One would have a somewhat lower-middle-class character, with families more nucleated, and with a greater degree of masculine dominance. The other would be a sort of "lower-lower" stratum of economically marginal people characterized by extended kinship networks and matrifocal household groups.

6.
Social Structure and Social Action

Of all places named as barrios in the city, La Laja has the clearest boundaries and in many ways the clearest existence as a community. In general, a named barrio is an area around some central landmarks; boundaries between barrios are vague, and a large barrio may include within it a number of smaller named barrios. But La Laja is spatially separated from the rest of the city; its boundaries are unequivocal. Its residents and the residents of other parts of the city call it a community. When its members sign a petition for electricity or to complain about a sergeant of the National Guard, they describe themselves as residents of Barrio La Laja. It has a junta which speaks in the name of the community, and although there may be those who do not feel as if the junta speaks for them, and those who take no interest in it one way or the other, no rival barrio junta makes its appearance. This is, further-more, a barrio in which there were attempts to solve a number of problems and to fill a number of lacks which were of interest to many residents; these attempts were often rather successful. It might be said, then, to be a good example of what the community development workers like to call "the community learning to solve its own problems by its own efforts."

I think that this generalization is worth looking at a little more closely. To what extent can a city neighborhood like La Laja be described as "a community?" And to what extent may it be possible for La Laja and barrios like it to deal with "community problems" through "community effort"?

There is no simple answer to these questions. I propose, rather than trying to make a single answer, to look at the situation from several points of view. I make of the general question three others: To what extent do the relationships among people in Barrio La Laja form a single, unified social structure? To what extent can Barrio La Laja, as a community, control noncooperators and troublemakers in its midst? To what extent and in what ways can Barrio La Laja be said to act positively to solve problems affecting its communal life? The answers to these three questions, while separable, will then be seen to have the same general tendency. La Laja, while not a place characterized by anomie or by social disorganization in the usual sense, is not the closely knit little community which the appearance of its brightly painted, densely built little houses might suggest. It has a great deal of community consciousness and a large amount of social interaction, but a degree of social cohesion less than might at first appear. Furthermore, the social institutions within the barrio lead out to, are part of, social institutions in the city and in Venezuela as a whole, and their functioning within the barrio is conditioned by that dependence.

An attempt to diagram the social structure of Barrio La Laja would fail to yield any clear pattern of social segments or of a social organization, formal or informal, effectively including the whole barrio. One would have to show the social structure of the barrio as the social networks of a series of individuals, forming a number of conspicuous large clusters, a number of smaller clusters, and leaving some relative isolates. Kinship is perhaps the main way in which these social networks are built, but the element of "choice" usually implied in the making of a sociogram is not absent even in the field of kinship. People usually choose kin, but which kin are chosen for continued association is a matter to a considerable extent open to choice. Moreover, the choice possible among biological kin is increased by adding to these real kinsfolk a group of fictive kinsfolk through *compadrazgo*. The result is the creation of a series of rather personalized social networks, rather than the creation of large corporate social groups.

There are other sorts of network formation within the barrio, still less formalized than those of kinship or pseudo-kinship. The people whose houses are adjacent to each other or fronting each other on the same street often form loose social groupings, especially of women. These groups are visibly present in the evenings, when people move their chairs onto the paved strips along the front of their houses and sit talking together while their small children play about. The proprietors of the community's small businesses become the centers of informal communication networks. They know many people in the barrio, establish relationships of *compadrazgo* with many, are important in opinion formation and organization of such communal efforts as community parties and the tree plantings in public spaces. One of the store owners is often seen reading aloud the news from the daily paper to anyone interested. Three of the four principal business owners are active in politics. (The business life of such shopkeepers is under a considerable strain through their social role. The evidence suggests that the giving of credit, which becomes a major feature in the maintenance of their social relationships, is a considerable drain on a business venture marginal at best; on the other hand, the case of a business which failed during my time of stay suggests that the proprietor who is unable to establish himself as the axis of many personal relationships is unable to compete economically with those business owners who can.)

There are also several active voluntary groups in the barrio. One is made up of the converts to Protestantism, conspicuous through their attendance at meetings both in town and in the barrio, their loud singing of hymns, and their marking of their houses with Protestant emblems. Other groups are associated with the various political parties. Their conspicuousness and group cohesion are strongly affected by the political situation in the municipality. When I first arrived in the barrio, the only group in public evidence, and that very strongly in evidence, was the group of Acción Democrática activists associated with the party then in power both nationally and locally and plugged in to whatever the local government had to offer in the way of assistance to the local community. The party had established its *mandado* or agent in La Laja, and through its control of the municipal government it arranged to put in his charge a small gasoline generator to give the barrio a source of electric light in the evenings. "Community development" efforts were generally being organized by the AD activists. Once the holding of a national election had resulted in the emergence of a two-party government in town, with members of the more leftist Union Republicana Democrática party sharing the municipal council with AD, the partisans of URD in the barrio in their turn emerged into the open of barrio life. They now began to extract favors in the form of truckloads of fill for a little baseball field and gravel for communal construction from *their* contacts at "city hall." Eventually, they were able to use a crisis over the building of a sewer to take over control of the barrio junta.

But these emerging groupings have not yet come to dominate a social structure still very loose and, considering the physical mobility of the population, perhaps long to remain so. In many interviews about the problem of quarrels and social friction I was unable to get anyone to point to any definitely recognizable factions in the community or to any long-standing feuds. Quarrels there were in plenty, and the two-party structure just emerging in the barrio by the time I left might with time coalesce into factions, but the social structure seemed to be too fluid to take this form yet.

Another way to ask "In what sense is La Laja a community?" would be by examining the problem of social control, of what happens to deviates and troublemakers in La Laja.

One way of describing the situation as to informal social controls in La Laja is to say that the social structure is too loosely meshed to cage anyone, that it is generally impossible to mobilize in the community a group large enough or united enough to force any sanction on the deviate. He who is disapproved of is disapproved of by individuals and clusterings of individuals; they may stare and they may talk, but the obstreperous individual will still find others to be his supporters, and he will be barred from no community facilities.

Moreover, in the highly personalized social structure of La Laja, an attempt to express disapproval of another's behavior can not appear in such a social context as to be read as "social sanction." It is perceived as personal disagreement and quarrelsomeness, and as such is subject itself to social disapproval. A family "of respect" is one which "doesn't get involved" in quarrels with its neighbors.

The ideal of being a family "of respect" which "doesn't get involved" in fights is not an easy ideal to put into practice. People in La Laja live so close to their neighbors that their radios and domestic quarrels are bound to be heard. Their numerous and undisciplined children are continually impinging on their neighbors by petty theft, stone-throwing, and simple invasions of privacy and peace. Many families keep domestic animals which roam into others' yards. The technical and economic level of living is such as to make for a constant stream of petty borrowings of ice, small food items, and small money loans. More serious still, the weakness of the conjugal relationship means that a husband or wife is fairly likely to find some neighbor presenting a sexual rival. Thus, it takes some effort to be a family which "doesn't get involved."

Certain social techniques have been developed to make this easier. One is that of using children as intermediaries. That it is always a child who comes to borrow a lime or an egg or to ask to buy a *medio*'s worth of ice from the lucky owner of a refrigerator might be seen as a particular instance of the general practice of having children run errands at the store. But the fact that a child is sent to ask a favor—a car ride to town for a sick family member, for example, or, bearing a small, closely folded note, to ask for a loan of money—seems to be a way of avoiding either an embarrassing refusal or direct hostility. Another technique is the general practice, at least by parents who take the child-rearing role seriously, of immediately disciplining a child seen annoying a neighbor.

Aside from this, there is a strong and explicit reluctance to say anything to a neighbor who may be carrying on some annoying activity. An example may illustrate. During my stay, the little junta supposed to represent communal needs in the barrio and to organize group action to solve them carried on a long discussion of the pig problem. The problem was that the pigs in the barrio, instead of being kept penned, were left to wander about to scavenge as much of their food as possible. They made the streets and public spaces dirty and disorderly. There was no difference of opinion within the junta over this situation's representing a problem; on this all agreed. The question was: What to do about it? Long discussion proposed action by the police, San Félix sanitary authorities, etc., but failed to present any clear means for ensuring that the pigs would be penned. A young American community development worker listening to the discussion was nonplussed. "Well," he said, "you say there are only six pigs in the barrio now, and two of them belong to one person. That means that only five families are letting pigs roam. Why don't you just go to those five families and in the name of the community ask them to pen up their pigs?" The suggestion was greeted with general and total rejection. "Oh, we couldn't do that."

Other examples of this kind of situation show the lack of local social machinery for controlling the noncollaborative, the annoying, the offensive, or the immoral.

When a considerable group of men were working as unpaid volunteers to finish the barrio's water line, there were other men in the barrio who took no hand in the work. Some sat playing cards in plain sight of a team working away in the hot sun. They did not appear ill at ease in the situation, nor was any attempt made, that I could see, to sanction them for their nonparticipation, beyond a friendly invitation to join the job.

One man in the barrio, otherwise liked and respected, formed the habit of playing his radio at top volume every morning from about 5:00 A.M. until he left for work at twenty minutes to six. Although several neighbors spoke to the writer of their annoyance at being thus awakened every day, and although (perhaps because?) on good terms with the radio's owner, they were unwilling to speak to him about his conduct. Similarly, when the bar played music late at night and again early in the morning, and when one evening a group of people experimented with a loudspeaker emitting ear-splitting racket into the street, no one felt it proper to object (until, finally, I did in the last case—and had my plea immediately and courteously heeded).

A young man in the barrio began to drink one week and, as his mood built up, to make gross remarks to his neighbors, especially the girls. His state and his remarks were the subject of general comment and of very strong disapproval, but no attempt was made to take him in hand.

A man on my street found it quite possible to leave his wife, seven months pregnant and with three older children, and to start living with another woman in the same block, refusing to contribute in any way to the support of the first family, although his wife's landlady was threatening eviction for nonpayment of rent. His conduct was certainly regarded generally as irresponsible and reprehensible, but the social disapproval was not such as to make him either help his wife pay the rent or move further away with his new woman.

A corollary of the weakness of informal social controls in the barrio is the fact that when people *do* "involve themselves" in quarrels with their neighbors, they are quite likely to call in the police. The woman owner of the bar across the street from me was adamant in her determination to avoid disorderly behavior in her bar, and should any drinker resist when she proposed to eject him she would not hesitate to go into town and get the paddy wagon, be the obstreperous young man one of the local boys or not. Of the five cases in which to my knowledge the police were called into the barrio in the first year of my stay (before the bar came in to bring with it a somewhat higher incidence of police intervention), only one involved the arrest of someone from outside the barrio (an attempted housebreaker) on the complaint of an insider, and three involved disputes between kinsfolk, one of whom called the police to arrest the other. The first of these was a case in which a woman called the police to protect her mother by arresting the son-in-law who was beating the mother. In another case a woman had the young son of her husband's first cousin arrested for throwing a stone at her. The last of the cases was one in which a young man called the police to arrest his common-law wife. The police may be called not only to deal with the personal but to deal with what looks, at least, like the trivial. The houseowner behind me threatened to call the police to arrest a neighbor whose little boy had thrown a stone making a hole in his thin sheet aluminum roof, an event not only minor but also very common, owing to the conjunction of very thin roofing with a passion for stone-throwing by little boys.

The barrio council, in asking the police to patrol the barrio in the evenings, especially on weekends, to keep down noise and disorder from intoxicated young men, was not proposing an enforcement method strange to the barrio. The lack of well-organized mechanisms of informal social control makes it natural for the barrio to resort to the impersonal mechanisms provided by the larger society, even in fairly trivial or rather personal cases.

What would have been new in the arrangement proposed by the barrio council was the community-interest framework of the enforcement. Indeed, the development of a barrio council may be looked at from one point of view as a groping toward some way of dealing with individual behavior from a level more general than that of personal opposition.

There was during my stay an outstanding exception to the general rule, a case in which the community succeeded in ejecting a family who had become generally disliked. Yet in looking at the history of this case, several points become apparent which are not in contradiction to the general thesis of La Laja's dependence on the institutions of the larger society. It took a long time and a great deal of provocation for the community's opposition to coalesce; informal gossip and interpersonal sanctions failed to do the job; and the exclusion of the unwanted family finally involved a community meeting and petition, which would serve to depersonalize the opposition, and the publicizing of these through the town newspaper and radio station.

The head of the unwanted family was himself a representative of external authority, a sergeant in the Guardia Nacional. His social role as "guardia" was much in the forefront of attention. Not only was he always to be seen in heavy-booted uniform and armed with a gun, but also he did not hesitate to refer to his right to "command" when crossed or annoyed personally. He was known in the barrio always as "the sergeant." While the woman with whom he was then living was disliked for being quarrelsome (she had been subjected to some sanctions through the failure of her neighbors to pay visits of condolence on the occasion of her bearing a child stillborn) and her children were disliked for theft, it was the guardia's insistence on using his policeman role in personal disputes with members of the barrio which at last brought community pressure to focus against him.

The barrio had been six weeks without water in the public faucets. When water began to run in the line serving the barrio, after a period of being shut off, it turned out that the local line was clogged, and it took many hours of unpaid work by volunteers from the barrio to get the line running again. At last the water came on, and as it did so, at five in the morning, "the sergeant's woman" attached her hose to fill her water barrels. This was all quite according to proper custom, but when some five hours later she still had her hose attached, her neighbors, hoping to attach their hoses before the water would be shut off for the day, had become frantic. It was rumored that the "sergeant's woman" was even doing a wash in the house (instead of washing in the river). People climbed up and peered over the wall to corroborate this report. At ten, one of the barrio leaders, the man who had done most of the work in repairing the water line, detached the sergeant's hose, and allowed another family to attach theirs. The sergeant promptly went into town and got the municipal police to arrest and jail the man who had removed the hose. Delegations of La Laja residents went to see the commander of the Guardia Nacional post across the river, and various individuals began to try to use whatever influence they had to get the arrested man out of jail. He was, in fact, released within twelve hours. Meanwhile, the Venezuelan community development expert in the barrio, who had led a protesting group to the municipal police station, had been put in jail for "lack of respect," and there he remained for two-and-a-half days.

A number of La Laja residents were surprisingly clear verbally about the issues involved in this affair. Some of them verbalized the issues to me as follows: The sergeant had been wrong in using the forms of law to serve personal interest. In getting the La Laja citizen out of jail, through personal influence, only the personal problem had been solved; the rule of law still had not been satisfied. "We in Venezuela do not have real laws yet." But the affair would have died a natural death, if a couple of weeks later there had not been a recurrence. This time the sergeant was stimulated by a quarrel with the Venezuelan community developer to attempt to arrest both the latter and the citizen with whom the hose issue had arisen—an attempt balked only by the two men going into hiding. In their absence, the sergeant did succeed in getting the town office of the National Transit Authority to impound the truck belonging to the community development team. This time there was a community meeting and petition to the sergeant's commanding officer, declaring the sergeant *persona non grata* in La Laja. These moves were organized chiefly by the group in the barrio tinged with URD politics, but had a somewhat wider base than they might otherwise have had because the solid and much-respected citizen first arrested had always been closely identified with the group of Acción Democrática activists. But even so, the barrio opposition did not feel it possible to use barrio pressure alone to sanction the sergeant. They addressed themselves to his commanding officer, and they arranged for the town radio system to publicize their protest.

There is, for La Laja, thus a problem of enforcement arising out of what the people of La Laja call *personalismo* at all levels. The loose social structure of the community leads its residents to call on the outside enforcing institutions for sanctioning their neighbors, but that same social structure means that the appeal to outside enforcement is more likely to come about in terms of personal grievance than in the framework of some sort of communal interest. At the same time, the outside enforcing mechanism is itself "personalist" in functioning.

Over the last years there have been continuing and not wholly unsuccessful attempts to develop a *community* organization in Barrio La Laja through the efforts of people within the barrio and outside it. This effort has been seen both by La Laja and by the outsiders as an attempt to develop in the barrio a capacity for "the community to solve its problems through its own efforts." Indeed, Barrio La Laja has been a model "community development project" of several groups simultaneously and has in the process achieved some small degree of fame, if mentions in *Time* and *Reader's Digest* magazines constitute such.

When my family and I arrived in the barrio, the house across the street from us was occupied by two young American volunteers from a privately supported community development group called ACCION. They had been living in La Laja about six months, had built with some community help a court for the game of bowls popular in Venezuela, and were in the process of helping the barrio build a water line. One or more volunteers from this organization were working in the barrio during the whole period of my residence there. Even before the Americans arrived on the scene, and conjointly with their organizing efforts, the barrio was among the projects—and often cited as a model example—of the community development branch of the national planning agency CORDI-PLAN, working locally chiefly through the Acción Democrática party structure.

The two groups—ACCION and CORDIPLAN—operated rather differently. For an extended period their different strategies and bases of operations made for a complementarity convenient to both.

ACCION was an organization started by an American and was American-run at the top, although by the time I left Venezuela it had moved from an all-American volunteer staff in the field to a mixture of Americans and Venezuelans. It derived its support primarily from the private businesses in Venezuela and operated quite independently of the framework of government services. The organization enlisted and trained volunteers and assigned them to the field to live in the low-income barrios of Venezuelan cities, paying them a rather small living allowance and giving them the task of "helping the community to solve its problems through its own efforts." The volunteers received a certain amount of supervision, but were to a large extent on their own, so far as defining the nature of this task in detail. At the time I arrived in La Laja, the organization was relatively new. The early group of volunteers were mostly rather young and without extensive experience or training in community development, since the organizers of ACCION were only themselves developing their program.

CORDIPLAN's community development program, in contrast, used almost no field staff of its own, but operated through stimulating, coordinating, and partially redirecting the work of persons already connected with the community as the staff of various agencies of the national government. Indeed, it would not be too far from the truth to describe CORDIPLAN's community development staff as one woman—intelligent, tough, drivingly energetic, and with excellent access to the ear of the president. She was nominally in charge of several hundred "community development" projects like the one in La Laja, which she kept going through occasional visits to inspire, bully, and cajole the locals. At least in the cases I was able to observe, CORDIPLAN's community development program had an obvious—and I thought, useful—tie to Betancourt's Acción Democrática party, for which it served as the beginnings of a local ward organization. The party in the barrio was fed by patronage in a rather socially desirable form—materials for community centers and water lines—at the same time that the community development format advertised, and made more generally accessible, the channels through which the man in the street could get help from the agencies of the national and municipal government.

The collaboration between the Americans of ACCION and the CORDIPLAN-Acción Democrática structure had its honeymoon in the building of La Laja's water line. The water line project was surefire from the standpoint of community interest—a solution to the community's most clearly felt problem. In solving it the Americans' resident organizing staff and the access to the financial and material support of the American companies in the region neatly complemented the local politicians' better abilities to use the municipal resources. The people of the barrio got not only running water in public faucets (at least for a few hours a day on most days), but a great big work party ending in a communal feast which they organized to celebrate the occasion. The mood was euphoric.

Immediately after the water line was completed, it was decided to hold a formal dedication to turn on the water. It was further decided that this formal dedication should be held in the old, now unused, schoolhouse, which would now become a "community center." To effect this arrangement the group of men from the barrio most active in organizing the laying of the water line constituted themselves, with the agreement of the American community development organizer, a provisional community junta.

The form of the formal dedication should have suggested something of the political situation to the American. Speakers at the dedication were all major figures in the town's Acción Democrática party organization. But the American was young, inexperienced with politics, new to Venezuela, and still speaking Spanish, although capably, with some effort, and he only identified the speakers' list as representing—as it did also—persons identified with community development in the town. Shortly thereafter, he began to pressure the provisional junta to call a general barrio-wide election to elect a new, more democratically selected junta.

The members of the provisional junta were, in effect, the Acción Democrática activists of the barrio; the president of the junta was the *mandado* or official agent of the party in La Laja. The more the American pressured, the less did the provisional junta or its president seem inclined to step aside and throw their posts open to elections. Finally, after months of this, pushed to the wall by the American, the president agreed to call a barrio meeting to ask for elections. At the meeting the president demonstrated that if he had learned nothing else from Americans, he had learned how to maneuver within the rules of the game of parliamentary procedure. One of the low-status members of the Acción Democrática party rose and made a speech urging that the provisional junta retain their posts; the motion was made and voted on, and the provisional junta stayed in power.

The young American was almost insupportably bitter at what he saw as a "double-cross" and as an unacceptable injection of politics in what he thought should properly be apolitical. The open confrontation focused the anger and sense of alienation of the young men identified with the party out of power, one of whom the American had hoped would be a major leader in a new junta. The Acción Democrática party leadership was equally bitter toward the American for trying to unseat their man. For a considerable time after the break, "community organization" was at an almost complete standstill in the barrio, the community center unused except for a daily distribution of milk for children under the auspices of the Ministry of Health and an occasional abortive attempt to "organize something" by one or two other leadership groups. The American was cut off from the support and assistance of the local politicians in power and found himself forced to rely on the companies alone. The Acción Democrática leadership was deprived of the support which the American community development group had given in the form of help from the American companies (considerably better capitalized than the local government) and of encouragement of collaboration from non-Acción Democrática young people in the barrio, and it proved incapable of compensating for this by its own efforts. Indeed, the AD *mandado,* while retaining his position as president of the junta, gradually took less and less of an interest in the barrio and eventually moved to another part of the city, returning only for occasional formal meetings forced on him by his party superiors. The "community junta" practically went out of existence.

But although the community organization was moribund, communal activity was by no means lacking. Petitions were sent in asking that the barrio get electricity, and after some negotiation the national electrification agency brought in electricity. There were a number of community parties—refreshments, sack races, climbing the greased pole, toys for children. Adult education classes were held in the schoolhouse at night for some months. Trees were planted in the open spaces, tended, and watered. A vacant lot was converted into a children's playground by planting trees and constructing two merry-go-rounds out of large scavenged wheels set in cement. A substantial cement-block building was erected to take advantage of an allotment in the state budget which would provide the barrio with a free meal every day for some fifty children.

Some of these activities were brought into the barrio by outside agencies such as the Ministry of Education, which organized the night classes for adults. Some were organized by small groups of individuals in the barrio; the playground was entirely the work of two men, and the parties typically were mobilized by three or four people who would then collect money from the rest of the community. The demand for electricity was organized by a group of men identified with the Acción Democrática leadership. The "children's breakfast" building was a collaboration. That the state had budgeted such a program for La Laja was, I think, an outcome of CORDIPLAN interest in the barrio. I used my contacts with the Corporación Venezolana de Guayana, the government development corporation in the area, to arrange for that agency to provide building materials; the organization of the work was done by a Venezuelan ACCION volunteer; and the rest of the labor was provided by people in the barrio generally friendly to him and to the left politically of Acción Democrática. They were not helped by the old group of "community leaders" identified with Acción Democrática.

These were in some sense "community activities" and might be described in the words of the community development workers as "the community learning to solve its own problems by its own efforts." I think, however, that the case of La Laja shows the inadequacy of this formulation to sum up the facts of social action in an urban barrio or perhaps in any community in a complex society.

The community does not have to act as a whole to initiate

procedures for solving some general problems; all it takes is a sufficiently active and influential working segment. Two men build a playground; ten sign a petition; three go to put pressure on the municipal council; thirty lay a water line. An undue stress on developing organization "representing the whole community" may actually make it harder to get things done by forcing individuals to choose sides, rather than choosing between action and inaction in a given enterprise.

There will be few issues which bear equally enough on everyone to make them matters, strictly speaking, of "community interest." Water came closest to being such an issue. Electricity probably came second in generality, but not a close second, for many people in La Laja cannot afford to pay for installation of a regular system; the substitution of the city system for the little barrio generator previously in use meant that nearly a quarter of the houses lost the elecric light that they had had before. Services for children are of interest only to those who have small children and who feel unable or unwilling to provide the service through their individual efforts. I believe the largest "barrio meeting" I ever saw in La Laja did not exceed sixty-five participants.

The community has, of necessity, only limited power to solve its own problems. To "organize a community" like La Laja often seems to mean putting together a structure for action which can plug in to some set of outside resources. This is, then, the building of political bridges between the barrio and the municipal, state, and national institutions which can provide what people in the barrio want. Venezuelans often deplore the entrance of nasty "politics" into community development, but the alternative seems often to be organization as ritual, powerless to effect action.

A local community in a complex society may in the end find itself powerless to solve what it sees as its problems because the solutions lie at points which they cannot control. Control must be both technical and political. A group formed to solve the community problems of the neighboring barrio of El Roble dissolved after spending a year in fruitless negotiations to see if it could not put in a water line. The gap here was not political but technical. It turned out that the system in use could not supply an additional line; the barrio would have to wait until completion of a new aqueduct being begun by the national government. A small barrio at the farther end of San Félix spent a year trying to get a school built, but was unable to do more than arrange to have a municipally-paid teacher give classes in a vacant house; they could plug into

the municipal political institutions, but to construct a school building they had to get permission from the national planning and
development agency, which was outside their control and which
vetoed the new school as part of a freeze placed on city building
pending completion of urban planning.

The "problems of a local community" may appear hardly relevant when the interests of a larger social unit are under consideration. The extreme case would be the community which was,
before La Laja, CORDIPLAN's model example of "community
development" in the city; this barrio succeeded in laying its water
line and getting in electricity, but was then demolished when the
national planning and development agency put in a new dock and
warehousing area. The people in the community near the dock
were quite realistic about this. They understood that the dock,
serving the entire region, took precedence over "their community's"
"community problems." Had there been in existence the political
bridges which would have enabled them to make contact with the
national development agency, they might have made some token
protest, but I think they would have accepted the destruction of
their community. They tried to use me as such a political bridge to
get more prompt payment for their houses in the area, and had
their means been more adequate to the purposes, they might have
achieved that. The interest which they might successfully have
pursued would have been that of the residents as individuals, not
as "the community."

If the idea of "the community solving its own problems" is a
generalization covering such a complicated lot of institutions, problems, and processes, why is it in such general use by both community development experts and by local community leaders? The
idea was in general use in all those "community activities" I saw in
La Laja, diverse as they were in objective and in organization. As
to the rhetoric in which the formula figures and the situations in
which the rhetoric is used, I have come to think that it may be
considered as functioning as what anthropologists call a myth: a
formulation which exists to validate action in the present. It provides an intellectual framework which gives moral validity to the
pursuit of wants and the balancing of interest between various
groups. It is, furthermore, an intellectual framework within which
people may compose their marginal differences and present a
common front. The human species seems to find politics difficult at
all levels without ideology; this is perhaps the minimum example.

This view of community development in La Laja as myth or

ideology suggests that the "community development movement" in the underdeveloped countries may have an interesting political role. This is, of course, not its only reason for being; it has practical functions as well.

In underdeveloped countries characterized by a shortage of capital relative to labor, communal effort has a clear economic role as a way of mobilizing surplus labor to build up such infrastructure investments as roads and water lines. The people of La Laja who complained, while digging a trench to lay their water line, "there are machines which could be doing this," were recognizing the difference between their situation and that in many other under-developed nations. La Laja also mobilized labor otherwise unem-ployed, but here this function appeared less important than it might have elsewhere.

In Venezuela as in southeast Asia, projects carried out by local communities can also fill another sort of practical gap—that left by the inadequacies of administrative structure which make it difficult to get the capital out into the field. Even an underdeveloped country which could afford to be building schools and sewers by governmental action may find it difficult to mount the programs to get the structures built, and in such a case "community develop-ment" may be in actuality the most efficient way of getting rapid action.

But to look at the phrase "the community learning to solve its problems by its own efforts" as ideology suggests another sort of role for community development. This is a role in helping to build in the developing countries new political and social institu-tions. La Laja did not build a water line, a baseball field, and a center for giving children free breakfasts just "by its own efforts." But by defining these activities as "the community solving its own problems," the organizing leaders in each case were able to mob-ilize enough group pressure to establish new channels of connection with the centers of power outside the community, and new skills in making such connections.

In the process they were beginning to develop a new kind of politics. The people of La Laja already participate in the political process. They keep track of political news through the newspapers and radio; they go to political meetings; they talk politics. But the political processes in which they participate in this way are those of ideological politics.

The community development movement in San Félix began, while I was there, to evolve into a kind of ward organization moving toward the sort of thing we know in the United States as machine politics. At one time there were eight barrios in San Félix where "community development" activities were going on. These various barrio community development groups were loosely controlled by the Acción Democrática structure in the town. In some cases the local leaders were local party activists; in other instances they were individuals only loosely connected with the party structure, but tied into it by the payoffs—in materials, in technical help, in public approbation—which the municipal government could provide. This embryonic "ward" organization evolved to the point where the various barrio leaders were brought together in the center of town to discuss their common problems at a meeting chaired by the head of the local government—an AD party leader.

I was astonished to observe that shortly before the national election, all this "community development" activity dwindled to an almost complete halt. I could not understand it. I still do not entirely understand it, but it may be that the correct explanation was that given to me by a ranking local party leader, a highly intelligent man educated in Europe. "In Venezuela," he said, "we still have the idea that you win an election by giving speeches, and before the election everybody was out giving speeches instead of getting on with organizing the barrios."

7.
The Sewer Controversy:
A Case History

This is the story of a controversy: of a fight between Barrio La Laja and the Corporación Venezolana de Guayana. The fight—which involved violence—was about a sewer, but more general issues were also clearly involved, and because these are interesting issues I shall tell the story in some detail.

La Laja is part of a developing city; it is also part of a city the development of which is being planned by professionals, both Venezuelan and American. The first is very much in the consciousness of the people of La Laja; the second is not.

Although most of the people of La Laja had heard of the Corporación Venezolana de Guayana, or CVG, they did not, in general, conceive of the Corporación as a general planning agency, the growth of the city as the outcome of its planning and development strategy, nor themselves as the subjects of such planning.

The people of La Laja, at the time of which this treats, had come in contact with the Corporación chiefly in two ways: as an employer or potential employer in the steel mill, which was the largest single employer of La Laja residents, and as a potential land seller in the nearby residential developments. Recognized as a possible special contact with the Corporación, I would be asked to use my supposed influence for two kinds of service: to help the petitioner get a job at the steel mill or to help the petitioner get a *parcela* (a building lot) in one of the new developments. (For both, a personal contact is very useful; however, I was not in a very good position to supply such contacts.) The general city planning and development activities of CVG had not affected La Laja directly, since La Laja was in a geographically marginal position off the main traffic lines and away from any main centers of population or industry. The general development and planning activities were the origins of various large constructions, such as roads, which were conspicuous to La Laja residents, and of a general prohibition on private construction making for general tightness in the housing market, which was reflected in a pressure on housing in La Laja; but neither of these phenomena was understood as part of general city planning.

There are several reasons for this. In the first place, much of the economic and physical development in the area had been undirected and uncontrolled by the Corporación. Although the steel mill was operated by the CVG, the two iron mining companies had preceded and were independent of the CVG, and although the CVG had begun to lay out roads and housing in some areas and to restrict or prohibit unplanned construction, a considerable proportion of recent construction in the area had been independent of or even counter to CVG city plans. Second, the various offices of the Corporación—at the steel mill, at the dam, in the free city adjoining the U. S. Steel Company town, and on La Laja's side of the river in the adjacent barrio of El Roble—represented the CVG as a congeries of particular functions, such as running a steel plant, operating an electric power plant, selling or renting residential lots in particular areas, rather than as a unified planning and development operation. Third, to the extent that the CVG had actually engaged in developing a city according to plan, it had done so piecemeal and locally. Complete plans had not been developed at the time of which this account treats, and the residential areas being developed by CVG appeared as unarticulated dispersed efforts unrelated to any over-all city plan, to the local population, and to those not acquainted with the planners' drawings. Many people in San Félix, asked by an interviewer to designate the location of the "new city of Santo Tomé" (of which, from the CVG or city planners' point of view, San Félix with its barrios like La Laja forms a part) indicated "the houses of Vivienda Rural"—a small housing development of new houses built by the Ministry of Health under CVG financing and supervision. Fourth, the general development planning and urban design functions of the CVG were being carried out far away from the people of La Laja, on the thirteenth floor of the Shell Building, 350 miles away in Caracas. Some individuals in San Félix—the priests, certain political and economic leaders—from time to time made visits to these offices, but to my knowledge no resident of La Laja had ever been there, and certainly the overwhelming majority had no conception of that far-off world in which La Laja appeared on maps as an area encircled by the planners' "Magic Marker" or zipatone symbols. The development agency was locally controlled by a political party with a minimal base in the region, and so tended to be even more separate than it might otherwise have been from local municipal institutions. Finally, the CVG, partly because of its physical and social distance from "the people of the site," and partly following a deliberate policy not unrelated to the foregoing, had greatly limited its efforts to acquaint the people of the locality with the agency's plans for the area.

In 1964, however, La Laja came into confrontation with the planning and development agency over a sewer. How this came about and what came of it is interesting in a number of ways. It might be looked at as a case history of the relation of planning to its clients or as a case history of the political process in an underdeveloped country trying to make its way toward democratic procedures after many years of rule by dictatorship.

Off the planners' payroll at the time of this controversy and with two and-a-half years' residence in the barrio and an identification with it in which the property owner's self-interest was mingled with emotional ties to a certain community and class, I naturally was drawn, in a situation of conflict, to the side of the barrio. I took part in the "Great Sewer Controversy" then, as a resident of La Laja. But it would not be fair to say that I took part in the same way as any other resident of the barrio. I had a special relationship to the planners, of which I tried to make use, and the other members of the barrio who took part in the controversy also tried to take advantage of my special position as *"Doctora,"* as a member of the *gente buena,* as a contact with the planning and development agency. The ways in which I was generally useful to the barrio and the ways in which I was uniquely useful help to illuminate the processes of which these ways were a part.

La Laja has been described as a very small "community" with a maximum amount of community consciousness but a minimum amount of social cohesion. Its residents are very conscious of being residents of a community with a special history and a special place in the world. At the same time they have never had a well-functioning organization representing the community as a whole, and the patterns of social relations are such as to make it possible for people to live as neighbors without getting deeply involved with one another. It is a community which finds it difficult to create continuing structures of long-term community action, but in which spontaneous movements directed towards goals of general interest can arise without much difficulty.

The issue around which the following events center was to a superlative degree an issue suitable for the emergence of such a movement, because it had to do with the barrio water supply. At this time, the only parts of the urbanized area with an adequate residential water system were the two company towns of the U. S. Steel and Bethlehem Steel companies and the little "camp" of the CVG near the dam site. Other parts of the urbanized area had water lines of a more or less provisional or intermittently functioning nature; but much of the urban area was dependent on water sold from tank trucks at one bolívar for a fifty-gallon drum and whatever access to the river each could afford. When I first arrived in La Laja in 1962 the barrio was in this last category, that of the areas without running water. Very shortly thereafter, it moved by its own communal efforts into the slightly more advanced level of areas with some water lines. The first Sunday I spent in La Laja I spent helping a group of some forty residents dig the trenches and install a pipe to bring water into a dozen public water taps in various parts of the barrio. This effort was the outstanding example of successful "community development" endeavor in the community. No project undertaken in the subsequent two and-a-half years aroused anywhere near the same level of community enthusiasm and participation. There may have been issues of more long-term importance to the residents—I myself felt that such an area was education—but the water problem was the outstanding area for felt concern. And the installation of the water line did not remove it from this area. In the first place, there were days or even weeks when water did not arrive in the so-laboriously installed pipes. In the second place, even when there was running water coming into the barrio it would run for perhaps two to four hours out of the day; people had to wait their turns to fill their barrels; and the idea of water for such large-scale usage as real bathing or washing clothes would have been quite out of scale. Bathing and laundry were still done in the river, and the river, as a bathing and laundry facility, was shared, as mentioned earlier, by La Laja with the residents from other areas who would walk several miles carrying their clothes in great basins on their heads. The water coming out of the public taps was thought of as "clean water," suitable for cooking and drinking, like the bottled drinking water which families in the capital bought to supplement the notoriously polluted supply in the taps.

One day in the middle of April 1964 some trucks and construction machinery passed through La Laja, went down the dirt road past the lagoon, and unloaded equipment and workmen at a point on the beach a little less than half-way between La Laja and San Félix proper. At this point they began to install a large sewer outlet. The pipes terminated exactly at the water line—then, just before the rainy season, at its lowest point.

People of La Laja, of course, immediately became aware of the sewer construction and began to discuss it in worried tones. The outlet would be somewhat downstream from the beach most used for bathing and washing; but the river current at this time of year was weak or nonexistent near the shore, and what there was of it tended to eddy back upriver toward the area most used for washing and bathing. There was indignant discussion of the pollution which would be caused by a sewer exit on the beach; it was said that in the rainy season the stagnant lagoon which forms behind La Laja would be a sink of sewage, that at all times of year the current near the beach would be insufficient to remove the wastes, and that children would get sick and die.

An informally organized antisewer group began to coalesce in the barrio. Among the most active and visible leaders were the people at this time most active in community development enterprises such as the building of the "children's breakfast center"; these were, in particular, a couple of brothers (the younger only seventeen) whose sympathies were predominantly URD or to the (legal) left of the government in power, and the two members, one Venezuelan, one American, of the privately financed community development team then working in La Laja. Members of this informal group went to the representative of the Ministry of Health in San Félix (he expressed support, but said he had neither cognizance of, nor control over, the project), to members of the municipal council, and to the newspaper, and organized a well-attended barrio meeting at which a statement of protest was drafted to be read over the local radio. Both newspaper and radio gave publicity to La Laja's apprehensions over the sewer. I myself visited the old and new heads of the chamber of commerce; the new head came and took a look at the construction site and agreed that a sewer at that point would ruin the only town beach, used not only by La Laja but to some extent by more middle-class types for bathing.

There was a buzz of concern and a movement of protest. But it was quite undirected. The first protests were aimed, via the newspaper and radio, at the world at large, or to whomever it may concern. In this they followed a common Venezuelan pattern; in Caracas, as well, newspapers, radio, and sometimes roadside signs direct the attention of the "competent authorities" in general to some local problem like a failure of water supply. In fact, people did not know who, in this case, were the "competent authorities" to whom complaints should be directed.

Some six weeks earlier I had heard a rumor—from a young American working in the American group under contract to the Corporación de Guayana—that a sewer was planned for this area. I had asked a couple of the consulting Americans who happened to visit me in the Guayana to check on it, but had gotten no report; my contacts had forgotten to check. I felt confident that the sewer was connected with the Corporación's city planning activities, but whether it was being built by CVG or another agency was in question. When I went to the CVG urban development office on my side of the river to ask, the people working there disclaimed all knowledge of the project.

Meanwhile, people from the barrio questioned the men actually building the sewer and were told that the project was under the national agency in charge of water and sewers—INOS. This agency had no office in the area.

At the large barrio meeting organized to structure opposition to the sewer, it was decided to send a delegation to the state capital to protest to the governor. People in the barrio seemed generally to know that he held public audiences once a week, and the day following the meeting happened to be the day fixed. As often seems to happen, the persons selected to make up the delegation were persons of relative unimportance in the barrio status structure; the main determining factor appeared to be that of availability. The three men were the Venezuelan professional in community development, who was, of course, at the disposition of such a project; the younger of the active brothers, who had to return to Bolívar that day in any case to go back to school; and an unemployed worker, kin of the family owning the bar. I was added to the delegation because I owned a jeep and could provide transportation, and because as "Doctora" I would lend a touch of social status.

My social status was, in fact, useful. On audience days the governor (or his representative) will receive anyone, of any social level, and for any problem; many of the persons waiting their turns were people asking for charity. (In the absence of an organized system for giving welfare help to the destitute, it would appear that the state governor's office, like the town government of San Félix, has to operate in the welfare field on a personal and individual basis.) However, the quota to be received had been used up by the time we got there. More recently arrived individuals were getting audience with the governor, but these priority cases were persons of higher social status—as judged by dress and by the cases I recognized personally. The seventeen-year-old leader of the delegation went outside the office and by telephoning the governor's secretary and stressing the presence of a "Doctora" in the group arranged for us to be received.

There was a long wait during which one member of the group went to the offices of the INOS and of the Ministry of Health in the state capital. In both cases, the agency representative expressed support of La Laja's position, but disclaimed any knowledge of the project.

The little delegation from La Laja was at last received by a man whom they took to be the governor, but who later turned out to have been the governor's secretary. He was courteous, organized, sympathetic, and agreed to request a report on the project from INOS in Caracas. The student was to get the report in three days. (When he did, at that time, pass by to get the report he was unable to get any information from the governor's office.) The delegation, satisfied that it had done what it had set out to do, returned home.

The next day I made another trip to the CVG office across the river, was told a name to consult on my side, went there and connected the name with a young man who said that the sewer was a CVG project, that he personally thought it an outrage, that he had nothing to do with the planning of it, but that the engineers in charge from the Caracas office were that day down "on the site" and might be found by making inquiry at the urban development office of CVG across the river. He gave me the name of the engineer in charge and urged me to take action before construction went "too far."

The next day I made three trips across the river, trying to locate this engineer. In the process I became very conscious of the physical and economic barriers to getting into contact with the planners in the absence of any telephone system. Each trip took about two hours and cost about two dollars in ferry fares. On foot I would not have had to pay for the ferry, but I would have had a very long walk from the bus line.

On the third trip I located the engineer in charge. It was about eight o'clock in the evening, and I found him playing dominoes with three friends. I knocked on the door, asked for him by name, and he identified himself without getting up. I explained that I was sorry to bother him after hours, that I hoped we might make an appointment to talk during his working day next day, and that it was about the sewer presently being constructed on the other side of the river. "Oh, you must be from La Laja," he said. I agreed I was, and thus it was as "one of those people from La Laja" that I carried out the interview which followed. This clearly colored its nature. The engineer declined to make an appointment for some other time. He said we might talk now, and we did; he continued to play dominoes. I set forth the barrio's concern with river pollution in view of the importance of the river for washing, household water, and recreation and said that we hoped for some assurance that the sewage would be treated before being dumped, or that there would be an extension of the sewage pipe carrying the waste into the channel at the center of the river. He said that no treatment plant would be possible because the sewer was designed to carry the waste from only half the city, another line being projected for the center of San Félix, and because it was a temporary sewer to be replaced in seven years by a permanent one which would void downstream. He said that the river was already dirty; that if we needed it, they could run a line into the middle of the river or clear up to Puerto La Cruz on the Atlantic Ocean if we liked; that if there was danger of people getting sick from the river they could build a fence to prevent anyone from getting to the water. He asked why we were objecting now when it wasn't even built yet; he said that in Caracas elegant apartment houses were built near open sewers and declared that we should not involve ourselves in things which were none of our business. We were both angry by this time, and both showing it, but the tone of the interview was formally polite; neither of us raised his voice. I asked whether the chief planner of the Corporación knew about the project, since it was my understanding that the planners were currently working on several projects for beautifying the waterfront in San Félix. He replied that there was no reason for them to have anything to do with it: "They'll never build all those projects anyhow." At this I laughed and agreed that he might be right, but said that I still thought they might be concerned. There was a moment of silence; we both seemed to have run out. I said I supposed the only thing for me to do would be to go to Caracas and talk to the heads of the urban development and planning divisions of the Corporación. He said, "Yes, that's the only thing; the only thing you can do is to get me fired." There was another uncomfortable silence. I got up and said that I had best be going. At this point, for the first time, the engineer stood up and made the conventional Latin-American gestures toward a woman of the same social class; he offered to accompany me. I supposed that my references, by name, to his superiors had revealed my status position. I thanked him, but said my jeep was outside and I would not need his help.

I made my way back across the river, and driving home, met the two American boys of the private community development group. They bought me a drink, and I told them how the interview had gone. Their reaction was to speculate at some length on the possibilities of "blowing" the sewer. The main obstacle to such a course of action on their part seemed to be a lack of dynamite and of technical know-how, rather than of volition.

By the time I got back to La Laja, most people had gone to bed. However, a group of young men whom I knew slightly were drinking pop by one of the little food stands. As a group they were among the better-organized of the young men of the community; one was a student and the others generally had reasonably skilled jobs—two were members of the baseball team. I stopped and at their request told them the story of the interview with the sewer engineer. They also were angry. As none of us was in a mood for sleep, we all walked together down the beach to see how far the sewer line had gone that day.

The construction seemed to be going rapidly, and there was a great deal of heavy machinery about—two steam shovels and some other equipment. The young men looked about for the inevitable guard. He was sound asleep on one of the steam shovels. We wandered about talking; he never twitched. With one accord the young men turned to pouring sand into the carburetors of the machinery. They seemed to know quite well how to do it. We walked home along the water and went to bed.

The next day I went to Caracas on the bus. I intended to discuss the sewer project, but as it happened I had been asked to come on that day to take part in a conference of American economists being brought down by the American consulting group to provide technical advice and, it was hoped, support on the development project.

News of the sabotage had reached Caracas, and the damage was said to be costly. It was reported that the contractor had insisted on having the national guard on duty at the site the next night and that on that evening one of the guards had fired his gun, although without hitting anyone.

One of the directors of the American planning consultant group was in Venezuela for the conference of economists, and I told him my tale of the sewer, hoping that he might be able to negotiate with the head of the development agency to satisfy La Laja's demand for an assurance that the sewer be extended into the river. Since he had hoped that one by-product of the conference might be a stimulus from the visiting Americans for better techniques of communication between the planners and the people, the visiting director decided to raise the sewer problem and sabotage episode as part of his talk opening the discussion at the conference, treating it as an example of an aspect of the Coporación's activities needing improvement. He did so. The meeting was formal, the "distinguished economists" from the United States being joined for the occasion by the top persons of the development agency. The latter, as well as some of the American consultant staff, regarded the visiting director's raising of the issue as an untactful washing of dirty linen in public.

I was removed from the program of speakers for the conference. Meanwhile, the engineer with whom I had had the catalytic interview sent a memorandum of several pages to his superiors in Caracas setting forth: a bacterial test showing the river already so highly polluted as to be unsuitable for human use; existing plans for an extension to carry the sewage into the channel; my "hysterical attitude" precluding an explanation of the facts on his part and presumed complicity in the sabotage; and a request that I—now identified by name, and thought by him to be an employee of CVG—be disciplined. The director of the American consulting group was put in the difficult position of trying to repair relations with the directors of the planning agency without retreating from a position which he felt to have been basically correct. Through a series of conferences with the Corporación's head and other officials he tried to negotiate this repair. He emerged from the last of these meetings believing that he had elicited a commitment that the head of the urban development division would himself meet with the "local people" about the sewer. In this, it turned out, he was mistaken; the head of the urban development division regarded such a contact with the local people as ridiculous and quite out of the question.

An approach was made by representatives of the CVG to the San Félix municipal council, and their agreement to the sewer project was obtained. Meanwhile, the sewer issue continued to have repercussions in La Laja. The police came to investigate, but made no arrests. The young man who had taken the lead in the sabotage of the machinery made contact with representatives of a national terrorist organization in San Félix and obtained a few sticks of dynamite to be used at a suitable opportunity. A young American working as a documentary photographer in San Félix at the time, worried by the increasing rumors of impending violence, but sympathetic to La Laja's opposition to the sewer, began consulting with the American community development team on the possibilities of organizing and publicizing a nonviolent demonstration in the barrio.

Meanwhile, the engineer in charge of the CVG urban development office on the site—perhaps on instructions from his superiors in Caracas—held a meeting to explain the sewer to residents of La Laja. He put himself in contact with the head of the barrio's community council, and asked that the latter call people together for such a purpose. Unfortunately, the council was at this period more or less moribund, and its head, the agent of the dominant political party, despite his clearly party-politician role, was a person of very minimal political skills who had been living outside the barrio for a year. He was so out of touch with recent events and so lacking in the political acumen to repair these deficiencies that he failed to gather together more than a handful of people for the meeting. (Besides a few La Laja people present at the meeting—I do not know how—was a young, leftish member of the municipal council of San Félix; it is to him that I owe my information on the conduct of the meeting.)

At the meeting the chief CVG engineer on the site appeared with the engineer in charge of sewers with whom I had had my interview. They were distressed at the small number of people represented, but made a presentation of the CVG point of view to those present. The sewer was presented at this time not as temporary but as permanent (indeed, the chief engineer told me later it had always been thought of as permanent), and as a necessity for providing sewage disposal to the new housing developments of the CVG in the neighboring barrio. It was said that a tube extension to the channel could be built. However, the chief engineer stressed, all this was in the long range unimportant, since a new waterfront development projected for along the Orinoco would eventually require the relocation of all La Laja's residents to better residential locations in other areas. The head of La Laja's community junta expressed satisfaction with the CVG's presentation. The agreement was reported in the local paper.

Whatever the merits of the junta head's agreement with CVG, its political inefficacy soon became clear when the more politically left faction in La Laja, already leading opposition to the sewer, convoked a well-attended barrio meeting largely devoted to excoriating the junta head for his public support of the project and general lack of contact with barrio points of view. They then organized a further barrio meeting in which a whole new slate of barrio junta officers was elected. The old head was, of course, not a member. More than this, the election represented a general turn to the left in La Laja's microcosmic politics, the old junta, basically the AD or government party in the barrio, being replaced by a group dominated by those aligned with the URD, the main party to the left of AD.

The newly constituted junta now decided to send a delegation to the CVG urban development office across the river to discuss their opposition to a sewer unless extended or the sewage treated. I was asked to serve on this delegation, I believe, for somewhat the same reasons I had been asked to visit the governor, and I agreed to use my access to the CVG office with its interoffice telephone line to set up the appointment. Feeling that after my scandal-making role in Caracas it might be more tactful to use an intermediary, I arranged for the CVG social worker to set up the meeting time. As I heard the conversation, the chief engineer was all amiability and at the service of the La Laja delegation at any time on the following morning.

The delegation was not identical with that sent to the governor, but similar to it, the Venezuelan community development worker and the brother of the seventeen-year-old leader of that delegation being on it. Also on the delegation was the new secretary of the new junta; it was at my suggestion that she brought a notebook and pencil to record the discussion.

Our little delegation had to wait for some time in the anteroom of the chief engineer. The wait did not seem to me unusually long, but it was long enough for the two younger men on the delegation to become tense and irritated. At last we were shown into the engineer's office by a young man with whom none of us was acquainted, who showed us to seats around a conference table extending across the width of the office at one end. The young man then seated himself at the head of the table, produced a pad of paper and a pencil, and asked us to explain our difficulty. Meanwhile, the chief engineer sat at a desk at right angles to the table where we were sitting and separated from it by a yard or so of distance and a free-standing screen; he appeared to be going through a pile of papers. Somewhat disconcerted, the two younger men on the delegation said that we had come about the sewer. "What sewer?" "Well, the sewer that is being built right near La Laja." The young man said that he was sorry that his knowledge of sewer problems was very limited, but that he would be glad to make a note of our problem. The delegation began trying to explain the situation, using a map on the wall.

At this point the chief engineer got up from his desk, apparently to leave the office, and in so doing passed around the screen and past our conference table. I greeted him by name and asked him if he could spare a few minutes to confer with us. He said that he was pressed for time, but might be able to spare us ten minutes. At this point, he moved into the place at the head of the table while the young man first receiving us left the office. The chief engineer opened discussion by saying that people who take little doses of poison daily eventually become immune to it, and that probably the people of La Laja were immune to sewage. As discussion proceeded, he explained that he meant to say that the beach could never be good for visitors and tourists because of the very high level of pollution existing in the Orinoco, but the rhetoric was not well chosen for the delegation from La Laja, who took him to be trying to say that the new sewer was by way of an experiment to administer the usually lethal dose, and said so. This contretemps cleared up, the engineer then turned to the Venezuelan community development professional and explained that he could talk to him, but that he could hardly be expected to discuss technical matters with people who could not even read or write. This rhetoric was not very successful either, the professional in community development, more sophisticated politically and probably further left than the other members of the delegation, being particularly annoyed.

Past this unfortunate opening rhetoric, the engineer turned technical, and from this point on conducted the interview in an exemplary manner. He set forth the need for the sewer to serve new housing developments being built by CVG, the existing river pollution, the plan to make an extension next year, the surety that the amount of sewage passing during the current year would be so small as to constitute no problem. He was also clear and explicit in trying to convey the institutional realities to the delegation from La Laja; he said that while an extension into the current was projected, he could not promise its execution on behalf of the agency because in Venezuela there is no continuity of projects and programs when people change; that he would try to get La Laja a connection with the new water aqueduct when it would be constructed, but could not guarantee the technical feasibility of such a connection, and that the same limitations on continuity applied. He agreed to have his office take bacterial samples regularly both from the river and from the lagoon and to make these available on request. The possible relocation of La Laja residents was not raised, either by the engineer or by the delegation; I do not believe that the delegation had heard of the proposed move.

The members of the delegation were satisfied with the interview and expressed their satisfaction. They also gave a favorable account of the discussion in a subsequent barrio meeting. I directed the council secretary in writing up minutes of the meeting and in sending a carbon copy to the engineer for his approval or correction. (This technique for lending some permanence to a verbally reached agreement was previously unknown in the barrio.) The young man with the dynamite felt somewhat balked at not being able to put the material to use, but was persuaded to hold off. Construction of the sewer continued, and the fight over the sewer died down.

A number of threads of the story were still left dangling. Would the CVG construct the sewer extension? (The chief engineer told an American interviewer that there were no plans for building it.) Would the barrio organization maintain its structure enough to demand of the CVG construction of the extension one year after the big fight? Would they actually go to the CVG office and request, and would they receive, the results of bacterial samples? To what extent would the behavior of the agency and of the local people build on learning from the sewer crisis to show modification in future confrontations? Another thread still dangling was the projected relocation of La Laja people in other areas. That this was not a unique invention of the chief engineer was supported by a conversation reported to me between a young American consultant and a Venezuelan engineer whom the American met on the plane to Guayana. The Venezuelan said that such a relocation was contemplated. But the young American could not remember the name of his informant; none of the other American planners had or could get any knowledge of such a projected relocation or derive it from any plans within their view; and my role as an agitator could not easily be changed back into that of interviewer of the Venezuelan planners.

It will be clear from this account that my role in the "Great Sewer Controversy" was such as justly to infuriate the top Venezuelan staff of the planning and development agency. I think that it was such, also, as to make it reasonable to look squarely at the accusation of some staff members that I was in some large sense responsible for what happened—that the issue would never have emerged if it had not been for "Doctora" Peattie.

In general, I believe that this accusation is correct. For something to become an "issue" requires more than that there be a problem of concern to a number of people. That is a first step only, and at least two others are necessary. There must be a process by which individual states of dissatisfaction are organized into the opinion of a group. There must then be a further process by which the group opinion is communicated, comes to that state of confrontation which we call "becoming an issue."

Looking at the process by which the sewer became an issue, I think it would be fair to summarize as follows: my role in the first stage, that of generating dissatisfaction, was negligible; my role in the second, of organizing the dissatisfaction, was peripheral or secondary to that of various community leaders, but my role in the communicating of the dissatisfaction was crucial. It seems quite unlikely that La Laja's dissatisfaction with the sewer would ever have become such an issue had it not been for my presence. The general protests by way of the newspapers and radio, the delegation to the governor, would have taken place even if I had never come to La Laja. Although I precipitated the sabotage of the construction machinery by reporting to the members of the barrio on my interview with the CVG sewer engineer, my influence here seems to have been catalytic more than generally causative; sabotage had been discussed in the barrio during the days before;

sabotage is a standard Venezuelan protest technique; it had been used before against CVG construction machinery in a working class barrio on the other side of the river. But the fact that La Laja's opposition to the sewer became a major subject of discussion, a big issue, in the Caracas office of the Corporación de Guayana was directly traceable to my intervention.

In looking at the history of the sewer controversy, it is clear that there were at least three major barriers to the communication of concerns from the people at the bottom to the "competent authorities" at the top of the system. These barriers to communication I suppose to be characteristic not only of the Corporación de Guayana, but also of other agencies in Venezuela, and not only of agencies in Venezuela, but of bureaucratic systems in similar societies around the world. These barriers to communication impinge on "the people" as lack of knowledge of the power structure, inaccessibility of the power structure in terms of time, distance, and financial cost, and social class barriers. I was very useful to the people of La Laja in dealing with all three classes of barriers.

It should be clear from the foregoing that one of the first difficulties experienced by "the people" in their wish to complain was their lack of knowledge of whom to complain *to*. In fact, the people of the barrio wasted a good deal of time complaining in general—into the air, as it were—or complaining to the wrong people: the sanitary engineer, the representative of the Ministry of Health, the state representative of the water and sewers agency, the governor of the state. Even when it became known—largely as a result of my somewhat more sophisticated investigative activities— that the appropriate agency was the Corporación de Guayana, the people in the barrio had no idea as to which part of the agency they should address themselves. Indeed, I had a long argument with one of my neighbors in which he insisted that we should go to the woman engineer in charge of allocating building lots in the nearby barrio of El Roble; she was, to him, the CVG, and I was quite unable to get him to understand that she would have neither knowledge of nor power over the sewer project. In the course of my participation in the sewer issue, I made some attempts to explain to other residents of La Laja the organizational structure of the development agency, but I do not believe that I was able to convey to any one of them a clear image of the division of functions that exists between the planners and the engineers, or between the central office in Caracas and the local offices on the site. The last was particularly difficult for La Laja to comprehend; that a person sitting behind a big desk in a CVG office, which they could see, had only the most limited powers of decision and often was not even adequately informed of plans for the area, made in Caracas, was something which they had no adequate basis for understanding.

The cost of communication in terms of time, distance, effort, and money is something of which I would perhaps not have been so aware if I had been merely an observer of these events; since it was my time, my gasoline, my bus and ferry fares which were involved, I became acutely conscious of it. It was partly as a rich woman that I was useful to La Laja. I had a jeep, I had time, I had money. Other people in the barrio had very limited stocks of any of these commodities. There was good reason why the members of delegations generally turned out to be people of secondary importance; usually, it is only the unemployed who can afford to spend a day going to the state capital or sitting in the CVG office waiting for an interview with the administrator. Then, all this traveling about costs money. It is especially expensive to communicate a protest when, as is true not only in Venezuela but in other similar societies, all the people with real power are in the national capital.

Finally, I was of unique usefulness to La Laja in being a person with some roots in the barrio who was, at the same time, clearly a member of the *gente buena*, a "Doctora," a person of upper-class level. When the head of the development agency was expressing—to the head of the consulting American group—his well-founded objections to what I had done, one of the things he said was that he could not understand how an educated woman, a "Doctora," could have behaved so. Partly this was a feeling that I should have come to him personally and shown personal trust; partly it was a conception of my role—which I did not share—as an agent of CVG in dealing with "the people." Part of this was, I believe, a feeling that I was somehow on the wrong side of a class line. A class system like that of Venezuela, formed in a pre-industrial economy, is reflected in the structure of politics and administration. To put it most simply, the administrators are superior not only in power and position but also in social class to those whom they administer, and their feeling about the social class difference is such as to suggest notions of caste. The chief engineer on the site found it quite possible to go to La Laja and hold a meeting to explain CVG's position on the sewer, but he found it intensely difficult to sit down at the same table with a group of delegates from La Laja. He found it difficult even though his social class position was nowhere near as high as that of his superiors in the organization, even though he had lived for a number of years in the area, even though he had ambitions in local politics. He found it so difficult that he had to tell the delegation so. At the same time, even though he had already asked that I be fired, when I greeted him and asked him to give us a few minutes, he could not treat me or my request rudely. The CVG engineer in charge of sewers did treat me rudely, but it was through ignorance; he had identified me as someone from La Laja, and therefore as a member of a lower social class. When the clues given in the interview caused him to change his identification, he changed his behavior. A person of higher social class might not count on having his protests acceded to; he can be relatively sure of having them listened to.

This social class barrier is particularly crucial because of another characteristic of bureaucracies in underdeveloped societies: the particularism of bureaucratic behavior. One student has described such bureaucratic patterns as follows: "The occupant of a post can make it his own personal province. ... If one has ties with prominent officials in the bureaucracy or is linked by kinship to key personages in the urban community or in the society, one is more likely to possess the freedom to act as he chooses. ... It is indeed expected that a bureaucrat will render aid to persons close to him at the expense of the general public" (Gideon Sjoberg, *The Preindustrial City*). In such a preindustrial bureaucracy, it is crucial to be able to establish a personal relationship with the bureaucrat, and it is precisely this which is made extraordinarily difficult for the person of lower social class by the status order of such societies.

In such a context an American bitterly feels the lack of the institutions and techniques of democratic politics which more developed societies take for granted. There should be, he feels, some congressman to get in touch with—some politician who can act as broker, as negotiator, to carry the protest from the bottom to the right man and office at the top. But there is none. The local politicians are very, very local indeed; their access to the power structure at the top, even within their own party, is hardly greater than that of the average La Laja resident, and they are subject in a not radically different degree to the same barriers. The members of the San Félix municipal council know nothing about the sewer and very little about the structure of the development agency, and they too feel powerless with reference to it. The national congress is in and of Caracas. There are some persons in town who have channels of communication to the state governor, or even to the national party structure, but these channels are weak and these persons are not accessible to La Laja. There is no one who is making his political capital out of the satisfactions and dissatisfactions at the barrio level except very local politicians, and the structure of institutions which would amalgamate these little local stocks of political capital into some sort of national party fund of support is still undeveloped.

In this institutional context, the propensity to violence in Venezuela becomes understandable. It is like the steam which cracks the closed boiler; it is a way of expressing dissatisfaction in a society which lacks the channels, the institutions, for protesting legally in any effective way. So first one puts up a sign by the highway or uses the radio to direct the attention of the "competent authorities" to the problem and then, if still feeling strongly, one looks for dynamite.

The particularism of the preindustrial bureaucracy affects the protestor in still another way; it makes it hard for him to get a firm commitment on the part of any bureaucratic agency. He may even find it hard to find out what agency policy is, because agency policy may not exist; it may be that various bureaucrats each have their own mutually conflicting policies. One member of the CVG views the sewer as temporary; another views it as permanent. One plans to resettle the people of La Laja elsewhere; another tells me that this out of the question. In such a system it is quite true that, as the chief local engineer told the delegation from La Laja, an agreement with one official one day does not commit the agency. A group treating with a bureaucracy having this particularistic structure finds itself in the same position as the United States government in the days when it tried—in vain—to make firm treaties with the American Indian tribes.

The process of public opinion formation in itself takes on a different character in the context of a system of institutions with this character. To distinguish various stages in the formation of issues—generation of dissatisfaction, organization of the dissatisfactions into a group opinion, and expression of the opinion—is not to say that these are independent of each other. People who see no possibility of organizing or expressing their dissatisfactions so as to change things may be unhappy; they will not experience themselves as being unsatisfied. In the process of organizing opinions, the possibilities for expression are formative. People shape their demands in terms of what is seen as possible. The lack of clear channels for expression and communication means that the formation of public opinion in a clear and definite form is itself rendered more difficult. The particularism of the preindustrial bureaucracy also has its effect on the processes of public opinion formation. When negotiations are to be carried on in terms of personalities rather than of posts, issues tend to be perceived in individual terms, rather than as instances of general principles. The conceiving of issues in this way contributes to maintaining the particularism of the institutional system.

The sewer controversy seems to raise another issue, not particularly tied to underdeveloped societies, although perhaps to be dealt with differently in such a society than in a more developed one. This is the issue which was raised when I asked the sewers engineer whether the planners knew about his project, and he brushed off their plans as *espiritista* projects which would never really be built. The issue is this: if the interventions of the administrators should be controlled in the interest of the publics whom they affect, should this control best be exercised through technical planning, or through conventional politics, or through what combination of the two? In this case, the engineers were reviewed neither by planners nor by politicians—but by which should they have been? This question in turn raises basic philosophical problems as to the conceptualization of the goals and methods of planning in the general interest. Do societies have what may be spoken of as a "general welfare" or is there merely a sum of individual welfares, aggregated as group interests? If one takes the first alternative, the development of political channels for complaint by such a group as the people of La Laja is not so important; one simply needs more and more effective reporters of local needs to the planners at the top. If one adopts the second view, the structure of political institutions appears as crucial.

8.
The World of
Señor Figueres

One of the things about a frontier city like Ciudad Guayana is that not only are people going different places, in the sense of shaping themselves different sorts of lives within it, but also that they have different origins both geographically and culturally. Some situations of social change can be described in terms of transformation along a single axis, of development away from a common cultural base. The situation in such a frontier city as Ciudad Guayana is not of this kind. If one were to speak of "life's race" here, it would be to speak of a race like the "caucus race" of Lewis Carroll's "Alice"; people are starting at various points and describing various trajectories of social movement.

The world of ideas and human relationships presented in the following pages is not, therefore, to be considered the cultural baseline from which all the various cultural levels represented in Ciudad Guayana have evolved. It is the intellectual world inhabited by one man, Señor Figueres. He is one of the semiskilled Venezuelans who make up much of the "working class" in Ciudad Guayana. The American labor relations expert, the Italian grocer, and the Lebanese hardware dealer are not only outside this world themselves, but they come from people whose past and present worlds were other ones. Even as an *obrero* Señor Figueres is not entirely typical. He is part West Indian; so too are many others, but

91

perhaps not most. He is an older man, and something of his stoic passivity may be understood best as an old man's view of life.

Yet because of the people whom I came to know well in the city, Señor Figueres seemed to inhabit a world of ideas least affected by formal education, mass communication, and urban institutions, because I came to know Señor Figueres well enough to understand a little the structure of this mental environment, and because the world of Señor Figueres came to serve me as a sort of baseline against which to view new inputs of ideas in La Laja, a description of his world may be useful to others. He represents a sort of adjustment to the urban-industrial world toward one extreme of a spectrum of real and potential adjustments. Because his adjustment is at one extreme, it seems to illuminate the processes of change going on there.

Señor Figueres is in his fifties, very dark skinned with that exceptionally rich color which comes from South Indian, rather than Negro, ancestry. He is of average height, but seems taller because of the dignity with which he carries his spare long-boned body, the deliberation with which he speaks, the formality of his manner.

When we came to Ciudad Guayana and moved into a mud-walled house beside the Orinoco, we soon met Señor Figueres. He was then living in the house behind ours, of which his mother's sister's daughter, who was married to a ship's cook of the Iron Mines Company, was the female head. Señor Figueres was working for this family, making an extension at the back of their house, and we arranged with him to build a wall around our backyard when he should finish. Thus, he came to be at our house every day. He came over every morning about six, not yet in his working clothes, to look over the job, and say, "Well, let's see if with God's will we can do a little work today," and go back to put on his working clothes. At the end of the day, he would make a similar pause for inspection, and a similar summary: "Well, we did a little bit today."

Señor Figueres' relationship to our family very soon took on other aspects. My husband and my son worked with him as mason's helpers, learning from him how to mix concrete and how to lay blocks in the local style. Meanwhile, he taught them Spanish. At this he was quite gifted. Not only could he still speak English from his West Indian days, not only was his Spanish slow, precise, and clear, but he liked to teach, to explain, to make clear. With me and with my husband, he soon developed a typical "anthropologist's informant" sort of relationship. He liked to talk about the world he knew; we liked to listen. From time to time we could reciprocate with information about the world we knew, and he liked that too. Thus, it came about that for some weeks, he spent almost every evening in our kitchen talking to us.

The world which Señor Figueres inhabits intellectually is predominantly a coastal world, a world shaped by water transportation. It includes Trinidad and other islands of the West Indies, British Guiana, the Orinoco delta, and the settlements along the Orinoco up to and including Ciudad Bolívar. But it also includes the oil towns of the vast plains which the Venezuelans call the *llanos*—Maturin and El Tigre, and their neighboring settlements.

Señor Figueres himself was born in Demerara. He has lived in Morawhanna—a town of British Guiana at the edge of the Orinoco delta—in Manoa in the Delta Amacuro proper, in Tucupita, the delta capital, in the oil town of El Tigre, in San Félix, and in the state capital Ciudad Bolívar. He has kinsfolk in Demerara, in Morawhanna, in Tucupita, in San Félix, in Ciudad Bolívar, in Barrancas, in several settlements of the Delta Amacuro, and in the diamond-mining camps at El Merey on the Caroní.

To travel about within this world does not seem to present any psychological obstacle to Señor Figueres and his kin. There are economic obstacles: the cost of the boat or bus or *por puesto* transportation. But cash once in hand, it is easy to pick up and go. Señor Figueres' sister in La Laja seeks medical attention in Ciudad Bolívar any time she is not flat broke financially; there is a free clinic in San Félix, but she prefers the big city hospital. Señor Figueres' mother spends time with her children in Barrancas, in San Félix, in Ciudad Bolívar, and at El Merey, according to convenience. Señor Figueres, at considerable expense and personal inconvenience and on borrowed money, traveled from Ciudad Bolívar south to Upata to see a doctor of whom he had heard well. Señor Figueres' sister, with several small children and minimal capital, moved herself and children from Tucupita to the diamond-mining camps in hopes of supporting herself there by selling snacks.

"It is good to travel around," says Señor Figueres. "One entertains oneself; the body needs travel; and when one goes about, one knows where to go and where to establish oneself."

But the larger world, outside this known one, is sensed only vaguely. To Señor Figueres, Caracas is known no better than the United States, and of the two, his curiosity about the United States is probably the greater. But he knows little about it. "Are there kings in the United States?" he asks. The world outside Venezuela appears in his mind as various cities in undefined spatial and social relationships to each other. One day he reported he had heard on the radio of fighting in "those parts"—in Philadelphia, or the capital of Russia, or maybe it was somewhere else. He firmly believes that the highest mountain in the world is in the Territorio Delta Amacuro; it is certainly the highest mountain *he* has ever seen, and he has climbed it himself and knows it is very high.

Like coastal regions the world over, Señor Figueres' world is one of racial mixture. His paternal grandfather was Chinese, and his paternal grandmother was what he calls a "coolie"—one of the South Indians who came in numbers to the West Indies. On his maternal grandmother's side he is Venezuelan. His mother's sister's five children are half what he calls "French"—Haitian—and to the "French" element he attributes some of a family tradition of "respect."

When Señor Figueres talks about his kinsfolk there is a tendency to be more definite with respect to ancestors through the maternal line. He knows that his father's father was Chinese, from British Guiana, but nothing beyond that; he has not only an idea of who was his father's mother, but also of her parents, although not of their exact names. His father spoke "coolie"—the maternal language—but not Chinese—the speech of the father. He knows nothing of any siblings of his father, but his mother's sister and her children are part of his known group of kin. The name Figueres itself comes from Pedro Figueres, the father of his mother's mother. Señor Figueres as a child lived with his maternal grandmother, since when the children were small the grandmother took her daughter and grandchildren to live with her, saying that she did not feel Figueres' father was responsible.

Figueres' first real liaison with a woman was when he was still in his teens. The woman was older than he, and he now regards her as a "bad one." It was for him an upsetting affair, and he was glad when it broke up after about a year. He has since been married twice, both marriages in common law. The first marriage lasted a long time. His wife left him just four days short of twenty-two years of married life. She said she had been thinking of doing so for some time. They had five children, and these were then old enough to be an economic help to their mother. Figueres says that the breakup of this marriage was a tremendous psychological shock to him, and for some time he thought he would never get over it.

But he did. "One must adjust." Some time later he married a girl much younger than himself; they now have two small children.

He says he has always gotten on well with his *mujeres* and conducted himself well. He cannot see why some people seem compelled to fight with their spouses. At the times when he himself had a girl "on the outside" he did not therefore quarrel with his wife. He tried to keep her from knowing, feeling that it was better to leave her unworried. He believes that husband and wife should conduct themselves "with respect" toward each other.

Señor Figueres was born in Demerara and lived there until he was seventeen. Although he rarely has a chance to use the English which he learned in Demerara, he still speaks it competently, and his Spanish has a precise and formal accent traceable to the West Indian English linguistic background. When he was seventeen he came with his mother, his brother, and his five sisters to Manoa, in the Delta Amacuro, the site at that time of an English mining concession. The family lived by farming—corn, cane, coffee—and occasional wage labor. For a few years he went to British Guiana, where he made a living as a smuggler. He then returned to the delta and continued farming. He was a married man with two children when he "finally got tired" of rural life and went to the oil camp at El Tigre, where his brother was already working with the American Mene Grande Oil Company. Both Figueres and his brother got technical educations out of the oil company; the brother was able to go to Caracas and start an auto mechanics shop, and Figueres learned carpentry and masonry as a company construction worker. In the early 1950's he came to Ciudad Guayana. Work was slow in El Tigre, and he had heard that there were jobs in Puerto Ordaz with the Orinoco Mining Company, then starting to mine and ship iron ore. He got a job with the company soon after arrival, but had worked there only a short time when the company sent him to the iron mine site at Cerro Bolívar. He stuck it out only two weeks. The foreman was a Spaniard whom he disliked so violently that he still speaks of him with great feeling; besides, there was a problem of hours; the work was away from the camp, often lasting until late, and by the time he got back to the commissary all the food was gone. Figueres returned to Ciudad Bolívar. He has never had a job with one of the big companies since. He worked for some time for an Italian carpenter, and there learned some skills which stood him in good stead later; he worked in the bar of a kinsman for about a year; he has worked as a master mason for various private individuals, both in San

Félix and Ciudad Bolívar. While doing various jobs he has lived in San Félix—he has lived there from time to time visiting his cousins—but he considers his home to be in Ciudad Bolívar, and he owns a house there. In 1962 he developed a serious rash on the arms which he considered was caused by working as a mason. He tried starting a small grocery in the building which he owned in Ciudad Bolívar at the outer edge of the sprawl of poor men's houses called the Barrio La Sabanita, but this soon foundered in a welter of uncollected and uncollectable small debts; he thought about starting another grocery on the main road between the ferry landing and Puerto Ordaz, but was unable to sell the building in Ciudad Bolívar to extricate his capital. Meanwhile, his wife was working as a domestic servant and bringing in the small amounts of cash which kept the family going at all. Figueres' ailment continued, and he borrowed money to see various doctors and buy medicines. No cure resulted. Figueres was going downhill fast.

In the days when Figueres was young, and in the rural settlement where he then lived, there were no free schools. Figueres' identity card says that he cannot sign his name. He can compute his earnings for a week at so many bolívares a day, and he knows the costs of various construction materials and with some effort can make a simple summation of costs of materials for a job. But confronted with the task of finding a half of nineteen, he was unable to solve the mathematical problem.

Señor Figueres knows how to mix cement; he does not know that adding water to the mortar mix to thin it later on will weaken the mix. He knows how to lay out a foundation, how to use a string to lay a wall level; how to place concrete blocks. He knows how to do simple carpentry. He knows how to plant the crops of the region—corn, sugar cane, rice, fruit. He knows what crops should be planted when the moon is waxing, and which ones should be planted when the moon is waning. He knows the names of many trees of the region and can give the use which can be made of each. He knows that trees should be cut for lumber when the moon is waning; when the moon is waxing the trees are full of water, and will rot if cut then. He knows about and is interested in the wild animals of the region. "Every animal has its intelligence," says Señor Figueres, giving as an example the way bees can make honey in the dark of a hollow tree. He also carries in his head sizable chunks of oral literature: tales, mostly of an exemplary sort, and some long poems written by a man in the delta and dealing with aspects of delta life.

Señor Figueres believes that learning is important. He sees formal education as crucial nowadays. "Before we lived in darkness; now we have light. Before everyone lived the same, he who had and he who did not have. Now he who is educated can do better." He feels that he himself missed the chances he might have had, first because he was not able to go to school, and then because an American who took a fancy to him when he was around eight and wanted to take him as a protégé was not permitted to do so by his mother, who did not want to lose her son.

Education, for Señor Figueres, is not only the material taught in schools; it includes all sorts of miscellaneous information about "the things of the world." He is proud of what he has acquired by traveling and seeing himself—the information about plants, trees, animals, the life of the Indians—which he could display to us. He is proud of his continuing drive to acquire knowledge from other sources, too, such as our *National Geographic*'s over which he spent hours poring. He says that he prefers motion pictures which give information. Here he cited one on the "Passion of Jesus Christ," and another, seen more recently, about Christopher Columbus, which showed how Columbus came in two ships with very big men who carried heavy sacks as though they were nothing.

It does not seem to him that he could now learn to read. His children will go to school and will learn to read.

The world of Señor Figueres includes entities which operate according to natural law and those which are subject to supernatural causation. There are "*cosas de la naturaleza*" and "*misterios de Dios*." That there is fresh water on Isla Margarita is a "*misterio de Dios*." Looking at a picture of an erupting volcano, Señor Figueres asked me whether a volcano was a "*cosa de la naturaleza*" or a "*cosa de Dios*." The volcano could be seen to be a "*cosa de naturaleza*" because I could give a naturalistic explanation of its cause. If one's car stops, one may find a mechanical explanation, and then one must of course repair the breakage. But one's car may just stop. It can be a spirit. Then sometimes if you turn your hat back to front it helps.

Supernatural causation is a more limited sphere than natural cause; it operates where natural cause does not rule. For example, says Señor Figueres, one can show the difference between a "*cosa de milagro*" and a "*cosa de naturaleza*" as follows: "If a person is born with some defect, it is very hard to cure, perhaps impossible." It is subject, in other words, to natural causation which supernatural agents cannot change. "But if it comes later, then perhaps it

may be cured by asking" (that is, praying). He does not characteristically think of the two sorts of causation operating simultaneously. Illness can be cured supernaturally in a few cases; in most it is
cured by vitamins and other remedies. Or one might try one and
then the other; he does not think of trying both at once.

There are plenty of people who can do witchcraft, especially
in Trinidad, but also in Venezuela, including plenty in San Félix.
Some are good curers, some do bad witchcraft. These latter learn
the art from books—such books as *Red Magic* and *Black Magic*.
(Books of these titles were observed for sale at the truck stop
between Ciudad Bolívar and San Félix.) It is a real study. The
good curers are cheaper than doctors, and if they really know their
business—there are those who pretend to but don't really—often
better.

Witches can fly across the river without support. They can
provide magic to make a husband tolerate his wife's infidelities, or
vice versa; to cause a husband to leave his wife when she wants to
take a new man; to make people ill; to make a party of people
quarrel; even to kill.

Supernatural causation can operate interpersonally without the
volition of the agent in the case of those people who have *mal ojo*
(evil eye) for animals, plants, and even for children. For such
people the living creature they covet sickens and dies. Once when
Figueres was a child he had a parrot which was *muy hablador*—a
good talker. A man came by to fetch water and admired the
parrot, asking if Figueres would not like to sell it. He put the parrot
on his finger and it climbed up to his shoulder very tamely. Within
a few hours the bird was dead. A child can be protected against
mal ojo by putting a certain kind of black stonelike material on the
child; then if the child is subjected to *mal ojo* the stone will split,
but the child receive no harm. A person who has *mal ojo* for a child
can give the child a little tap, making him cry, and this will
neutralize the effect.

Besides the human world, there are spirits. The *Sirena* lives in
the sea. Señor Figueres has seen her but only at a distance. She
passes in a very swift boat. She is said to be very beautiful, half
human and half fish. She is said by some to be a person who went
fishing on Good Friday. The *Duende* is like a human being, only
all hairy. He likes to steal children and carry them off. They become
all hairy, become *duendes* too. A small cousin of Figueres was thus
carried off and found miles from home.

Less definitely personalized are a host of other spirits for "everything has its (spirit) *dueño.*" "In the forest you may hear someone chopping, and there is no real person there. Or you may sense something passing. These are spirits." There are spirits in the river. One hears them laughing. They may trouble human beings or just leave them alone.

Señor Figueres knows some stories of how people were punished by supernatural agents for working during Holy Week. And there is the cousin who was carried off by the *Duende.* But in general, the spirit world is quite separate from the human one. Señor Figueres knows nothing of any patterns of behavior, so familiar in many primitive societies, for placating the spirit *dueños* when farming or lumbering. There is nothing which one should do with respect to the spirit *dueños.* And just as the "natural" explanation takes precedence over the *"misterio de Dios"* in the case of the volcano, the rational everyday world of the commercial town seems to repel the spirits. Ciudad Bolívar, an old regional center, has a spirit living in a rocky island in the river. But there are no spirits near San Félix; "there is too much traffic."

To Señor Figueres, who has no idea of any rituals or prayers connected with the traditional agriculture, it would surely never occur to put any prayers or similar rituals into such a task as building a house.

I have recorded two long stories told me by Señor Figueres. They are both about the same theme: worldly success. But they derive different conclusions with regard to this theme. The first tells how a man tries to fool his wife into believing he is "making *conuco*"—farming—when he is really fooling around. He is helped in the deception by (unseen and unpersonified) supernatural agents which actually get the work done. But he is finally punished when the same supernaturals pick all his corn from his cornfield and kill him. "This story," says Señor Figueres, "shows that laziness brings no good." The second story deals with what follows a bet between two rich men, one of whom argues that you don't need money to make money, the other that one can become rich "out of thin air." A complex series of events proves the latter right. But this story does not directly answer the arguments of the first, for the hero here is not lazy; he strives for success throughout the tale, but during its first half—the part where he is being given capital by the rich men—is continually foiled by chance events. His later fortune is equally due to chance.

I seem to see here an attitude which I have met many times among unskilled workers in Ciudad Guayana. It seems to be that expressed, for example, by a man who said to me, "Man always aspires to better himself, right?" and a few minutes later said that he imagined himself in future "going backwards, even though always aspiring to do better. It is different for the *gente establecida*"—the middle class. Man strives, and should do so; it is wrong to be lazy. But man does not have worldly success within his area of control; in the end, circumstances determine.

Working-class Venezuela has a proverb: "*El que tiene medio, medio vale*" ("He who has a nickel, is worth a nickel"). Worldly success is important. But life is hard, circumstances present themselves, and "*hay que conformarse*"—one must adjust. If one asks a man, "How are you?" he may say, "Fine," or "All right," but he may say "Here" or "*Luchando*" ("Struggling"), as though to endure were in itself triumph enough.

Although in Señor Figueres' world circumstances seem to rule man more than man can rule circumstances, circumstances should not be understood as static or unchanging. He clearly sees that his world—at least in its cultural and social aspects—has changed very much in his own lifetime and that it is still changing. He likes to talk about the culture of the Indians whom he knew in his boyhood in the delta: of their ways of house-building, of fishing, of courting, and marrying. But he sees these Indian ways as ways which are dying out: "The missionaries have been changing all that." Nor does he see these changes as undesirable. The technology from which he makes a living he sees as something which has changed in his lifetime; the whole tendency to build in cement blocks he sees as something of recent history; he reports that the technology of the carpentry shops, in which he has worked at various times, was completely transformed under the influence of Italian immigrants who taught the Venezuelans how to cut so as not to waste wood.

Señor Figueres also sees quite clearly that cultural and social changes of these particular sorts have been part of a more general transformation of his world. "In former times people wore *alpargatas* (the rural woven sandal) all the time. They put on *alpargatas* from the time they were born and grew old in them. Now you see everyone wearing shoes. In those days you might occasionally see someone going to or from Bolívar in shoes and a necktie but now everyone dresses that way." There were in those days, he says, two sorts of people: *los campesinos* and *los del pueblo*—country people and townsmen. But "now you see the girls all dressed up when they go into town. Many even know how to drive a car." He recalls in his youth visiting an isolated settlement and seeing a group of children hauling water in gourds; the children turned and fled, so unused were they to strangers. That would not happen now. People now travel to "*dar cuenta*"—to see things. There are schools everywhere. In the old days there were no schools, and the parents could not teach the children because they didn't know.

Not all change has been for the better, in Señor Figueres' view. The manners of modern children disturb him. When he was a child he was trained to be very "correct" in someone else's house. If offered food, he should say he had eaten. He would not look about, nor touch things, certainly not take things. The mothers of today do not keep enough track of their children. Children do not show respect.

But by and large Señor Figueres' view toward recent social and cultural change is positive. He conceives of these changes most generally as a widening of experience and knowledge, and as he values positively travel, learning, and other ways of widening experience and knowledge so he values positively the changes which have made it possible for the *campesino* to "*dar cuenta.*" It seems natural to him to say: "We used to live in darkness; now we have light."

Since he thinks that these changes have been a good thing, and since he sees them as resulting from specific human activities, in particular, the activity of the government in building schools, it might be possible for him to conceive of the changes as being "us" changing "ourselves." This is not so. He supports the government of Betancourt, and thinks of Betancourt as being "for the people"— but he does not imagine that he can have any control over the government. When I reported to Señor Figueres that an informant of mine in San Félix had predicted a Communist take-over in the government he looked very distressed and said, "Listen, Señora Lisa, here in Venezuela people have a tendency to talk in the air, to discuss things they cannot possibly know anything about. Only the government can know what is possible, what can be done. Those who know are the *técnicos*. Perhaps some of these *bachilleratos* know something. But a person who can't read, even less has he any basis for discussion. Let's make a comparison; you are the mother and it is your task to take care of the children in the house. Now they start arguing and want to do something but you are the only one who knows if it is possible; you have to decide."

The rich may have contact with the government; the poor, believes Señor Figueres, cannot. It is not the president's fault, he believes. The government, the president, send the money, but the local officials spend it on this and on that and pretty soon it is all gone; in Caracas, they believe that everything has been done. "If you are a rich man and go to borrow money you don't ask for a thousand, you ask for five or six and you can get it easily. But suppose you are a poor man, you want to borrow some money, they come and make an investigation and look around and see that you have nothing so they don't lend you any. The rich man always has his friends, and he can invite the official to a good supper, invite him to drink some whiskey. . . . If an official comes from Caracas he is pretty soon surrounded by the doctors and lawyers and rich people." I suggested that the poor might unite to exert pressure on the government. This Señor Figueres sees as impossible. "The Venezuelans are very disunited. If one wants to do a thing, another will say no, or want to do it in a different way and so no one does anything."

In the same way, in the changes which take place in cities Señor Figueres sees the poor at a disadvantage and as being pushed aside by the rich through a process which people like himself cannot hope to change. "Sometimes the poor man can fix up his house so it looks all right, but sometimes he hasn't the money—then he has to leave" when the rich move into an area. "It doesn't look well—suppose there is a nice house here and another there and between a house of earth. The government will help the rich buy it. For example, suppose they want to put a gas station there. So the poor always move to the outskirts. . . . Besides, the poor cannot afford to build on owned land. . . ."

Even "good" government, then, Señor Figueres sees as a government by people with other forms of power, largely economic, but also intellectual, which put them outside his control. Those who govern are not the servants of the people, or at least, not of people like Señor Figueres; they are people with power. People like Señor Figueres have no power.

Nor does Señor Figueres see the political process as operating in a framework of laws. "Here in Venezuela we do not have real laws," he says. "You hear of one today and the next day you hear nothing more of it." For example, in his barrio of Ciudad Bolívar there was a law that before building a house you had to have water and sewer lines, toilet, and so forth; then poor people could not build; "but then that was all forgotten and you could build without even a hole. So there are no real laws, because each is just made for the time and the next day the rule may be totally different."

Señor Figueres will never make a "modern man." He knows it, too. He lives in the city and likes the city, but his orientation is still more rural than urban. When he talks about the city, or about industries of the region, or of the companies that run them, he speaks about them as things which are largely beyond his comprehension. They are not observed and perceived with anything like the acuteness or the sense of comprehension with which the plants and animals of the delta figure in his talk. He knows he will not now learn more complicated skills. He will not now learn to read. His children may learn more complex, more urban, more modern skills. His daughter, he thinks, might even be a secretary.

Señor Figueres is a product of an underdeveloped country. But looking at the world of ideas in which he lives, it can be seen that—as such worlds go, the idea-systems of underdeveloped nations—his is not such a bad base for development.

Señor Figueres would not find it easy to travel far, to travel outside the boundaries of the region which he knows and where his friends and kin live. But within that region he travels easily. He is available for the labor market. As he once went directly from his cornfield on the delta to the oil towns of the *llanos* to seek a job in wage labor, he would move again at hearing of a job opportunity. In this availability, in this willingness to move, he appears to be typical. The growing city is full of people who made the jump from small farmer to wage laborer in town and who found—it would appear from their accounts of it—no considerable psychological barrier to doing so.

Unlike the Indians of the southwestern pueblos in the United States, unlike some tribal Africans, Señor Figueres is not called back from the town and from "modern life" by a tightly knit community which is holding a place for him. He lives in a social world in which ties to kinsfolk are important, but in which a particular set of or a particular structure of ties are not crucial. One wants to be with kin if possible, but except for the mother, one kinsman or kinswoman can more or less substitute for another. Nor is there a larger, communal system which needs him to make itself complete. There is no "Spring Corn Dance" awaiting his participation, no clan shrine at which he must sacrifice. Economic activity does not have to count here with this sort of competition.

Nor does economic activity, in Señor Figueres' world, have to carry an antirational burden of ritual and ties to the supernatural. The supernatural is in his world, but it does not interpenetrate much with the natural world. One sows one's corn, one builds one's houses, without ritual and without reference to the supernatural.

There is, besides, a positive valuation of experience and knowledge in his world, and of the rational and systematic acquisition of knowledge. Even the witches learn their witchcraft out of books as a "real study." The availability of free public schools represents to Señor Figueres a real and highly valued revolution of possibilities.

Finally, there is a general readiness to accept change. Señor Figueres is interested in change, rather than against it. The changes he has noted in his own lifetime are many. Some of them—in particular, those involving a loss of "respect" behavior interpersonally, especially in the case of children—he does not like. But many of them, especially those involving a widening of intellectual and economic horizons for people like himself, he values very positively. There is certainly no general tendency to look back longingly on "the good old days."

What this view of the world conspicuously lacks—from a development point of view—is the sense of control over the environment. Both individually and collectively as a member of the class he calls "*los pobres*" (the poor), Señor Figueres sees himself as subject to circumstances, as compelled by forces to which one may maneuver to adjust, but which one can hardly hope to change. "One should not be lazy" is the moral of one of his tales—but the moral of another is that, "after all, luck determines." He sees man as trying to "*defenderse*" (to defend himself) and to "*conformarse*" (to adjust). He sees man as trying to keep afloat with dignity in a world he never made and cannot hope to remake. The sense of being able to dominate circumstances, which is a psychological basis of saving for future objectives, of spending in time and money for education, of a rational calculus in which present satisfactions are weighed against possible increments of future situational advantage—this Señor Figueres' world lacks.

9.
The Intellectual World
of La Laja

"We used to live in the darkness; now we are coming into the light," Señor Figueres said to me, expressing his sense of being part of a society which is being transformed in ways which are more than economic. La Laja is part of an intellectually transforming society. It is diverse, and becoming more so; the young are learning things that their parents did not; and the community is continually receiving a variety of communications from a variety of sources. Radio and newspaper bring in reports of fighting in Cuba or of the assassination of a president in the United States. The primary school and special night classes for adults teach reading, writing, arithmetic, and the facts of Venezuelan history around which national identity centers. Sewing classes and an auto mechanics class teach manual skills. Into the barrio come the "community development" organizers, the saleswoman of Avon cosmetics, the missionaries of Jehovah's Witnesses. A sound truck passing through the barrio may herald a political meeting in town, or the arrival of educational films from the Ministry of Health, or of movies, shown in the barrio street, on "How to Build a Better House" from the Venezuelan Cement Institute in Caracas.

Of course the processes of intellectual transformation going on in Venezuela as a whole, or in the little bit of it represented by Barrio La Laja, are not identical for everyone. One aspect of the process as a whole is precisely that individuals within the society more and more learn particular specialized things, and that the range of difference between specialties widens. Even in a little barrio of less than five hundred people there are a large number of specialized sorts of information which only certain individuals carry around in their heads. Here is a trained accountant; there is a man who knows how to cure illness by laying on hands; two women are specialists in giving injections; a teenage boy is developing a specialty in bicycle repair; the owner of the bar is also a professional electrician.

So it is in some ways an appreciable falsification to speak of Barrio La Laja as constituting an intellectual world, a pool of ideas and information, into which pour the various communications from outside. Ideas do not distribute themselves uniformly like the molecules of a liquid in space. But even so, it makes some sense to speak of the barrio as a frame for the storage, communication, and reception of information. It makes sense because the barrio is so small and class distinctions within it are still so undeveloped that people are not shut off from communication with each other. While they cannot share all of each other's specialized knowledge—say of electrical repairs, or of the management of the dock at the steel plant—they can assimilate the existence of this knowledge into their social world, as something which people they know as persons have learned. They can also call on that special knowledge when they need it; if your record player stops working, you call on Martin for help; if you want to write up a petition in formal language, there are certain people who will be able to do it for you. To the extent that the people who have that knowledge are part of your social world, the likelihood that you will acquire the information yourself from them is enhanced.

At the same time it must be recognized that the barrio as a frame for handling ideas is not a box but a complex structure. The way in which information will be received and used will depend on the intellectual and institutional context into which it fits. Information comes from different sources and impinges in varying ways on individuals; it is seen as relating or not relating to various sorts of concerns. The social meanings which the communication has will determine how it is used. The following pages look at the kinds of communications coming into Barrio La Laja and at the social meanings which they seem to have for its inhabitants.

An inventory of the information being communicated in Barrio La Laja would have to take note, first, of a large and still quite current stock of traditional material. Such, for example, is the traditional technology of building the *bahareque* house—how to build the frame, how to mix the earth and straw for walls, how to plaster it on, how to whitewash. Such, also, is most of the technique of cookery. The musical arts of playing the *arpa, cuatro,* and *maracas* are part of the body of traditional knowledge, as are also many of the songs sung to their accompaniment, like the Christmas carols for which the state of Sucre is noted. There is a very large body of knowledge about plants—both flowering plants for ornamenting the home, propagated generally through cuttings, and wild and cultivated plants used for medication. There are such skills as the making of nets and the braiding of hammocks. There are magical arts, from the minor household ones like secretly putting a broom, straw-end up, behind the door when you wish a guest would leave, to the more specialized and dangerous techniques about which Señor Figueres told me.

These sorts of information are traditional in the sense that their origins lie in more rural and traditional ways of life and that they are generally communicated interpersonally outside the written word and the formal "teaching." People also think of them as different from official bodies of knowledge. One seeks herbal remedies by asking a neighbor; one goes to the hospital to get pharmaceutical drugs. They are not, however, universally disseminated any more than the more "modern" skills are. Only two men in the barrio, both from the northern coast of Venezuela, are really competent to make nets; not everyone feels himself competent to mix the mud and straw properly for a *bahareque* house. Furthermore, even these sorts of knowledge enter the channels of mass communication. There are cheap pamphlets on the magical arts and on herbal remedies for sale at the newsstands in town and along the highway. The traditional Christmas carols are recorded now, and the records are played on the bar jukebox during the weeks before Christmas; meanwhile, new popular songs, heard on the radio or the jukebox, enter the repertoire of the singers and *cuatro* players in the barrio. Thus, one of the intellectual consequences of the movement of rural people into the city is the wider dissemination of traditional cultural lore, both through the interpersonal contacts of people coming from places with different regional cultures and through the recording and codifying of tradition and its entrance into the realm of mass communications.

Mass communications also, of course, bring in the new. Jukebox and radio teach new songs; cinema, magazine, and newspaper depict new styles of dress and makeup, new dances, new sorts of behavior. Even the goods sold in the market are a kind of information on and enticement to new styles of consumption and of self-presentation. This process has gone very far among the Venezuelan *clase obrero*. Oil prosperity and the spread of mass communications have transmitted mass market consumption styles far into the rural areas which are the urban hinterland. It is not remarkable, then, that in La Laja mass communication "styling" dominates many aspects of life. Girls do their hair on roller hairdos in imitation of the latest fashion in Caracas or New York. Their dresses also follow the fashion to the best of their ability. The kitchen at the back of the house is likely to be dirty and untidy, lacking the "presentation" aspects so important to the North American middle class, but perhaps this is just because the housewives of La Laja haven't heard *that* news yet; the living room is almost sure to feature plastic upholstered furniture, a coffee table, plastic flowers and ornaments. There is, then, a revolution in styling, in self-presentation, going on, stimulated and directed by the spread of mass communications and of the cash economy.

When Señor Figueres spoke about "coming into the light" he was thinking of something else. He was thinking especially of formal schools. Like most rural Venezuelans of his generation, he grew up without access to schools. Of the small part of the barrio's population over sixty, eight out of ten are illiterate; half of those between forty and fifty cannot read or write. But the building of schools and the movement from farm to town is changing rapidly and radically the chances for formal education. Of people in the barrio from thirty to fifty, less than a quarter are illiterate, and of those under thirty only a handful cannot read or write. No one over the age of thirty in the barrio had gone beyond sixth grade, the terminus of primary school; seventeen individuals below that age had studied or were studying beyond the primary school level. One had entered technical school in Ciudad Bolívar. Almost all the children in the barrio are enrolled in school, although it must be noted that they attend with greatly varying degrees of regularity and intensity of application.

There is a small primary school in the barrio itself, its program covering grades one to four. It is housed in a new modern building of masonry with glass-louvered windows. But parents who take their children's education seriously complain that one of the teachers often arrives late or fails to come at all and that even for the grades included the school offers inadequate preparation. So since the town practices what would be called in the United States an "open enrollment" policy, children of La Laja go to school also in four other public schools in San Félix and El Roble. Some children of Iron Mines Company workers go to the school run by the company in the Iron Mines camp. A couple of boys go to the free Catholic boys' school in El Roble. Several girls go to the Protestant school in San Félix, and the two children of one family attend the Catholic girls' school which, at twenty bolívares a month tuition, is the most elegant offering in elementary education available on La Laja's side of the river. With all this coming and going, magnified by the fact that all the major public schools are on double shift, and dramatized by each school's distinctive uniform, the groups of school children coming or going on the road are a conspicuous part of the daily human landscape.

For the families of La Laja, sending children to school does not involve a choice between education and immediate income as it does in some countries, for the ways in which children can earn money are extremely limited. But it is not without appreciable economic costs. There is the cost of the school uniforms and shoes, and a cost, in soap and labor at least, of laundry; for while a dirty dress is acceptable for playing in the barrio, it is not so for attendance at school. For those who go to school out of walking distance, there is the bus fare. Finally, but not least, there is the cost of pencils, papers, and books, since schools neither issue books nor have libraries. Children whose parents work for the two American mining companies have their school supplies paid for by the company, but for other families the cost of books may mean a choice between nonattendance and attending school without books.

Children start school at ages which vary considerably, according to the exigences of their parents' mobility and circumstances at various times. Furthermore, they may drop out for considerable periods. In addition, the rate of repetitions in Venezuelan primary schools is, for a number of reasons, extremely high. There is, as a result, much less correlation between grade level and age than in North American schools. Children in one grade may differ over five years in age. I found a number of cases like that in which a thirteen-year-old and her eight-year-old sister were together in second grade.

In addition to the three R's, primary schools present material on personal health and hygiene, plants and animals, and on the geography and history of Venezuela, focusing very heavily on Simón Bolívar and the period of the Wars of Independence.

Teaching methods emphasize rote repetition and writing from dictation and copying, and stick very closely to texts. I was present at a sixth-grade lesson on economic development in Venezuela, one which had obviously been very thoroughly prepared by a confident-appearing teacher. It treated Venezuela's economic possibilities almost exclusively in terms of minable resources such as gold and diamonds, making almost no reference to development of manufacturing. Hydroelectric power was not mentioned. No reference was made to the steel mill or the Guayana development program. The mastery of both skills and "material" thus appears as a rather specialized undertaking, not connected with the experiences of everyday life.

This view of primary education is, apparently, implicitly accepted by both parents and children. Schooling is universally agreed to be a good thing, but what might be taught and how, and the possible adaptation of the content of primary education to the requirements of daily life, are not subjects of discussion. In part, this may be attributed to the lack of an institutional framework for such discussion, since schools do not promote the sort of PTA organization characteristic of schools in middle-class neighborhoods in the United States. But this seems to be, in turn, related to a lack of pressure from parents for controlling the content and style of teaching.

It may be that education in a country like Venezuela is not intended to relate to everyday life only—or preeminently?—as a way of providing skills and understandings with which people can perform their everyday tasks. If it is the latter, surely it is also something more. One goes to school in a clean dress not just to learn things, but also to become an educated person. In a country like Venezuela, which until rather recently has had a highly stratified class order with formal education associated with upper-class status, this is an exciting idea. To be educated is not just to have information and be able to practice skills; it is to conceive of oneself differently.

Both literate and illiterate persons often refer to the illiterate as a "*bruto.*" The sense is not that of brutality; it is like the use of the word "brute" in the English "brute beasts." It contains implications of lack of polish and refinement, perhaps even moral insensitivity. The word is apparently used much as the Russians, passing recently through a similar social and intellectual transformation, use the term which we translate as "uncultured."

There is, then, an aspect of formal education which can be

thought of separately from its functions in the providing of skills. It is access to the cultural activities "of respect," the activities associated with being a person who counts in the social order. It is in this way, I believe, that we are to understand also the books requested by a teenage boys' "sports club" in the next barrio when given a chance to start a little clubhouse library; they wanted, in large part, books of poetry and Venezuelan classics. In this way is to be understood also, I believe, the elaborate rhetorical styles used by barrio leaders at formal meetings; the "speech" is not just to state problems and propose solutions, but to provide an opportunity for *obreros* to appear with dignity. "Passing into the light" through education is a number of different things, but one of them is an access, on the part of working-class people, to styles of behavior which had heretofore marked people of higher social status.

Just as the education of the *gente buena* was focused on verbal and literary skills and their children went to the university to become doctors and lawyers, rather than engineers or chemists, the "respect" connotations of education in La Laja seem rather strongly focused on reading and verbalizing. The acquisition of technical skills like mechanics or dressmaking does not seem to be invested with at all the same aura, but is treated in an instrumental way.

That is not to say that people are uninterested in acquiring such skills, at a number of different levels. Dressmaking classes in the barrio, given by a teacher from the Ministry of Agriculture, were immensely popular. Several young people were taking courses at the Institute of Commerce; one was at the technical school; as I left one man was negotiating to enter the course in construction at the new government trade school. Others have learned skills from electricity to nursing through on-the-job training. ("Working with the company" has been, for the present adult working-class generation, the outstanding route to technical expertise.) The technically skilled recognize, and other people recognize, that they have improved their life chances and are worthy of commendation for acquiring such skills. Technical skill goes with other status-raising behavior like more middle-class styles of child rearing. But just as, at one level, it is formal education which requires that one of the *gente buena* be addressed by a title like *Doctora* or *Ingeniero,* so at the lowest level it is illiteracy which makes one a *bruto.*

Quite a different intellectual stream from the information communicated by schools is the area of news. The communications made in schools are handed down to be received, remembered, repeated. They are not to be discussed or manipulated or immediately acted on. News is part of the active intellectual life, and it is discussed, at times manipulated, and at times acted on.

News comes from various sources. The national newspapers are sold in town ond often read by residents of La Laja; even more seen in the barrio is the state of Bolívar newspaper, which has but spotty international coverage, but very good reporting of news of the town. As a source of other than local news the radio is the outstanding supplier; over half the homes in La Laja have radios. The town radio station also contributes, and with considerable effectiveness, to the spread of local news by news bulletins and by live coverage of local events. Finally, there are said to be "clandestine" radio stations which give news of Venezuelan political events not carried on the official networks—and of course from other than the official point of view.

So far as other than strictly local news is concerned, the focus of news reporting is on Venezuelan politics; the scene of the drama tends to be Caracas, but the context is national political events and trends. It is not surprising that the people of La Laja show almost no interest in "international events" per se; De Gaulle, for example, could hardly be said to have been heard of in La Laja. But certain international events are intensely interesting in La Laja. I came back to the barrio after a week's absence during the Cuban crisis of 1962, and meeting first one of my neighbors, a housewife whose main interest in life appeared to be her children and doing the wash, asked her, "What's new around here?" "Nothing," she said, "except this terrible situation in Cuba." I found that all over the barrio people were sitting in little groups around their radios, and that the crisis was the main topic of general discussion. When President Kennedy was assassinated, I was receiving condolences in La Laja within three hours after the event. But concern with these events was, I believe, no exception; they were seen as important because of the basically political focus of the interest in news, and since Venezuelan politics is seen as developing between two opposing poles represented by the United States and by Cuban Castroism.

News-making is a political tool, and "getting publicity" through the news media is a process well understood in La Laja. The barrio leaders involved in community development work generally took care to visit the correspondent of the *Bolivarense* to get him to report on their activities. When people in the barrio wanted to stop construction of a sewer outlet on their beach, they at once went to the newspaper and to the radio station and arranged to have their opposition publicized. At one time the small group of leaders in barrio activities associated with the further-left part of the political spectrum actually began to publish a small mimeographed weekly newspaper for the barrio. Their general aim was to build up identification in the community with the "community development" activities which they were promoting.

The relatively active treatment of the input of communications which we call "news" seems to relate, therefore, to its fit into the institutions of politics. It relates to the structure of a society which, although its political institutions are still undeveloped—and perhaps, one might argue, *because* its political institutions are still undeveloped, and politics still a game at which an amateur can play—has a fairly high rate of political participation. As La Laja's struggles over the sewer suggest, the participation may have a low rate of payoff—but it is still an ongoing activity, and it is this activity which shapes the use of news.

An interesting set of ideas is coming into Barrio La Laja in the form of Protestantism. Protestantism seems in the La Laja setting to imply something more than an alternative to Catholic religious belief and practice. To see why this is so, one has to look at the way both religious institutions are used in the barrio.

Most of the people of La Laja are nominal Catholics, but neither in the form of participation in the rituals of the organized church, nor in the form of unofficial folk Catholicism does their religious affiliation appear to play an important part in their lives. Everyone in the barrio, except the handful of Protestant families, is baptized in the church, this ritual following by several years on a home baptism not officially recognized. They also take First Communion and are buried from the church. Attendance at mass is uncommon, taking of communion rare. Very few people have been married in church, in part because the refusal of the church to recognize divorce under any circumstances is not congenial to the people of La Laja. The sacrament of extreme unction seems not to be in use. No one in La Laja, and no relative or friend of anyone in La Laja, is in religious orders or contemplating ordination; Venezuela nationally does not produce clergy to staff its church, and the priests and teaching nuns and brothers of San Félix who serve the people of La Laja are Spanish. To the best of my knowledge, there is not a single household shrine in La Laja, although a number of families have religious pictures on the walls of the *sala*. Most commonly, the picture is of "*el siervo de Dios*," a sort of officially unrecognized folk saint, a doctor known for his miraculous cures.

During the period of my stay, one family only, one year, erected the decorated cross traditionally set up in rural Venezuela on the fifth of May and used as a focus for singing and drinking. Prayer and lighting a candle to some saint is a recognized response to serious illness or to other trouble, but it does not appear to be a typical response, as it is, for example, in rural Mexico.

For that group of thirty or forty people in La Laja who have been converted by the *Evangelicos*, a fundamentalist Protestant group, the spirit of religious practice seems to be notably different. They do more participating; their participation is deliberately conspicuous; and their religion seems to make demands on them which cut very much deeper than in the case of the Catholic majority.

Part of this difference may be attributed to the recency of the *"Culto."* At one time in 1962 a considerable group of recent converts were trying to attend church in San Félix every night of the week and twice on Sundays. As the weeks passed, the intensity of their participation sloped off notably, to a matter of once or twice a week.

In part, the difference may be attributable to consciousness of minority status. During the more fervent period the *Evangelicos* held a number of street meetings in La Laja, with group singing of hymns. Later, they held meetings in dwelling houses, with loud singing and preaching evidently aimed at calling the attention of the unconverted outside. The *Evangelicos* paste large signs attesting their membership on the front of their homes. Even about the house the Protestants like to testify to their faith by loud hymn singing.

In part, however, the difference between Protestant and Catholic practice seems due to some basic differences between the two religious institutions. The Protestant church is led by Venezuelans. It offers its members a chance to participate freely and actively, not only in the singing which forms a major part of the group activity, but by "testifying" before the assembled group. Although the *Evangelico* service does not seem to run to the extremes of emotional expression sometimes seen in fundamentalist services in the North American rural South, it is notably a much more emotionally expressive affair than is the Catholic mass. From time to time there are conventions of Protestants from various parts of Venezuela, which offer one of the few opportunities a resident of La Laja is likely to have to travel as delegate to a national organization.

Even more important an appeal seems to be, paradoxically

enough, the stringent demands placed by the new faith on its adherents. *Evangelicos* are not only supposed to follow a strict sexual code, but are also not supposed to dance, drink, smoke, or go to the movies. A non-Protestant informant said that it was his understanding that some particularly rigorous *Evangelicos* lived only on bread and milk. When a young girl of the faith from La Laja married in 1962, the beliefs of her mother and of herself, to the dismay of her neighbors, allowed no party or celebration to signalize the occasion. She and the young man went to the prefecture to be married and then, after visiting her parents, went off to their new home with no further ado. In addition, the faith places intellectual demands. One should read the Bible and be prepared to explain its meaning at services or to people outside the faith.

All these requirements are not easy to live up to, nor are they felt to be. Indeed, their general emphasis on self-denial and control seems to go against all that is most characteristic in the way of life of the people of La Laja. Their stringency often repels people from the new religion. "I couldn't be an *Evangelica*; I like to dance too much." At the same time, their very stringency seems to be an important element in the appeal of Protestantism. Evangelism calls on the convert to enter a more demanding, and by the same token, a more bracing, moral atmosphere. It provides the exciting sense of doing a difficult, praiseworthy thing in the company of a supporting group.

The case of one man who was unable to live up to the demands may give some of the flavor of the movement, as well as of the position of the illiterate. In 1962 one of the most active converts in La Laja was a man of fifty-eight, an illiterate from a rural state of Monagas background. This man, although formally the *jefe* of a considerable family, was actually a person of little social position. He was perpetually unemployed, the family being supported by one of his grown daughters, and although an active member of the AD party in the barrio, not one of the looked-up-to managing group. When he joined the *Culto*, he regarded his conversion as the opening of a new life. He was seen every evening herding, like the lead goat of a flock of sheep, a group of women to meetings of the *Culto* in town. He told everyone that he had given up drink and women and was gaining against the ingrained habit of smoking. As time went on, however, he began to weaken. He expressed doubt that even "with the help of God," he would be able to give up cigarettes. Then one Saturday night he was seen drunk. The following week he left the *Culto* and appeared in my house full of depression and strong liquor. He reiterated again and again that as an illiterate he was nothing but a *"bruto,"* that *evangelismo* was a better way, but that he was too much of a *"bruto"* to keep it up, especially since he was too uneducated to read the Bible and testify.

Time will tell what will become of the Evangelist movement in La Laja. It seems likely that in some respects, at least, the movement will loosen some of its requirements and temper some of its demands. One might predict the invention of a "party" form approved by the *Culto*, presumably centered around other things than dancing and the drinking of alcoholic liquor.

On the other hand, if the movement continues strong, one might predict that it could have important social and economic effects. Although the notion of work as a vocation, characteristic of Calvinism, does not seem to be a part of *Evangelico* doctrine, in other respects its behavioral requirements are very close to those of the classic Protestant ethic. A man who cannot drink, smoke, dance, or carry on with women is, in La Laja, more or less left by default to work and save. In addition, the movement positively commands a struggle for self-control and self-education. A small piece of evidence for results of this is the following: an American supervisor of dock construction at the Iron Mines Company remarked to me that the Protestants in his work crew were the only members of the crew who kept working when he was not there. There may have been other—such as ethnic—correlates of Protestantism which were important here. Nevertheless, the Protestant movement does seem to have a kind of unique bite as a conversion experience which demands a basic reorganization toward self-discipline and self-improvement.

The people of La Laja, then, are "coming into the light" in a number of different ways. There are inputs of ideas which are simply additives, items widening the range of possibilities, without involving any basic reorganization of ideas. Modern drugs and medical techniques seem to be such additives. If you have a nail wound, you may treat it magically, by boiling the nail which cut you and washing out the wound with the water. Or you may treat the wound herbally, with an infusion from certain wild plants. Or you can apply a drug, like penicillin. The style of functioning of the hospitals, as dispensers of remedies, rather than as teaching institutions, has fitted in with the treatment of illness in La Laja as a matter of applying particular "remedies" so as to make modern medicine merely another set of medicines, available from a different source than the old herbal and magical ones.

Other changes are of a cosmetic nature; they make the person appear to his fellows and feel to himself "dressed up," "more modern" or "more cultivated." Such changes are involved in the adoption of urban styles of dress and hair arrangement by women, the building of houses which imitate, within the economic possibilities, the styles of the middle class, the furnishing of one's living room with upholstered furniture and plastic flowers in plaster vases. Formal education has a certain ornamental or cosmetic aspect of this kind. Such changes are superficial; they should not be underestimated for all that, since they may have very great symbolic importance and be essential in building the confidence and will to make other changes, or in validating other changes made. But they do not in themselves cut very deep.

Other changes in ideas are of the sort which involve the development of new skills and information relevant to the practice of the skills which enable people to take part in new institutions or to participate in new ways in old institutions. The learning of typing or welding is such a change. I suggest that learning the arts of politics is another. Here, too, no basic restructuring of character need be involved in learning the skill, but insofar as practicing the skill makes for a new kind of life, it may bring far-reaching consequences in its train.

Other changes might be called conversion experiences, in a way which would widen the use of the word "conversion" to include gradual transformation in ideas of the self, as well as the sudden vision of change which overturns the old self in a moment of revelation. There are no doubt secular conversion processes as well as religious ones. However, a religious cult like the Protestants in La Laja offers a convenient framework for conversion because of the combination of prescriptions for change with a superrational validation for change and a mutually supporting group of converts.

All these sorts of processes are going on in La Laja. If La Laja is "coming into the light," it is through an uneven, complex set of intellectual changes, sometimes appearing as separate items, sometimes fusing together into more general movements shifting life styles and conceptions of persons.

10.
Some Paths of Becoming

In former times, said my friend Señor Figueres, speaking of his own childhood as of an epoch far off in the past—the coming of oil has made it seem a different world—there were two kinds of people in the country, who seemed clearly distinct from each other. There were *los campesinos* (country people) and *los del pueblo* (townsmen). The difference between townsman and countryman in style of life was expressed in conspicuously different styles of dress; Señor Figueres finds it easy to identify the two groups as those who wore shoes and those who wore the local sandals called *alpargatas*. Now, as he clearly sees, there are no longer two distinct kinds of people. "Now you see everyone wearing shoes." Girls from the country, he says, appear "all dressed up when they go into town. Many even know how to drive a car."

In Venezuela urbanization is not something which is happening only in the cities. Roads, radios, newspapers, schools, imported goods, have penetrated the countryside. In the city these communications are, no doubt, received with greater frequency and impact, but they are reaching outside the cities too. These communications, added to a "traditional," rural way of life already loose in social structure and intellectually oriented toward the practical and material, mean that those who now come to the city come in some sense

118

preadapted to urban life. One observer has called them a "proto-proletariat."

This means that in La Laja one does not see the kind of transition which anthropologists report for some other countries undergoing the first stages of modernization—the jump in stage which happens when the tribesman, the blanket Indian, the peasant, move to town. The people who come into the cities of Venezuela are not wholly raw recruits; they have already put on the uniform of modern life. And, as every army knows, the uniform makes a difference.

We might, for convenience, distinguish four stages in mobility. In the first stage migrants into Ciudad Guayana have already in general passed the level at which people are directing their efforts toward the satisfaction of traditional wants through traditional skills exercised through a traditional manner of organizing the self individually and interpersonally.

The second stage would be that in which the fountain pen appears in the illiterate's pocket, and the transistor radio in the Indian's hand. People learn to have new wants, and they look for cash income to satisfy them; but they try to satisfy these wants through the manipulation of traditional skills, or of these skills relatively little modified.

In the third stage people begin to focus on the exercise of skills as a way of coping. The child says, "I'd like to be a doctor." The parent says, "I want my son to go through school and get educated." The satisfaction of the new wants begins to be thought about as an aspect of "being" another sort of person, with a different bundle of skills.

However, it is possible to think about being another sort of person, in the sense of enacting another sort of social role, without at all conceiving of how to organize the self so as to be able to enact that role. So, among New York City school children there are differences between lower-class and middle-class groups in the matter of aspirations—truck driver versus doctor—but these are less striking than a more subtle difference which also emerges very clearly; the lower-class child, even if he has such "middle-class aspirations," characteristically is very much less ingenious than the middle-class child in seeing connections between what he is currently doing in school and what he would like to see himself doing later on. The middle-class child seems to see himself as creating himself as he goes along; the lower-class child sees himself as an actor, but not as the subject of his action, not as training himself.

There seems to be a fourth stage in the mobility process: a stage in which the individual sees himself not only as satisfying the new wants through new skills, but as acquiring the new skills through a sort of shaping of the self.

In La Laja, no one—except perhaps the *Indiocito* who goes out to fish from his shack up the beach—is still in the first of these "four stages." On the other hand, one sees there only the rudimentary beginnings of the last of them. The deliberate shaping of the child's character by the parent, and of the individual through his own future-oriented education and self-discipline is barely beginning to be seen.

The dominant life-style in La Laja is very far from stressing self-discipline—or discipline by others—and the frugal deploying of resources over time in pursuit of long-range ends. Bars in San Félix characteristically have on their walls a sign asking for *Orden y Respeto*" from their customers, but "order and respect" are what the people of La Laja are always complaining that Venezuelans lack: "We Venezuelans are very disorderly," they will say. "There is a lack of respect." People show lack of "order and respect" by drinking, by being noisy, by using profane language, by quarrelling, by allowing their children to roam the streets freely for much of the day, by using intimate forms of address to their *compadres* and *comadres* and to their elders. All these forms of behavior are common.

As far as drinking is concerned, for example, it is notable that masculine social interaction—and there is a good deal of it—is generally accompanied by drinking of beer or, more expensively and less commonly, rum. A community work party, to lay a water line or build a building, also calls for the support of beer and rum. By the time a group of men from the barrio finished the day's work involved in laying a concrete floor in the children's breakfast center, they were so drunk that the chief mason found it more practical to wield his trowel from a somewhat waving kneeling position than from a standing one, and other members of the work party were dancing drunkenly on boards laid over the still-damp cement.

In this life-style children participate along with adults. While the mason waved his trowel sinuously over the floor, a group of boys aged from ten to perhaps fourteen were enthusiastically scrounging sips from the rum bottle and cavorting about in a manner which suggested that the rum was having a considerable effect. When my little girls attended their first children's birthday party in La Laja they were astonished to find that the only element familiar to them was the cake, which was brought out at about ten-thirty at night. Rather than consisting of the sort of "children's games" played in New York, the party consisted otherwise of dancing to music provided by an extension loudspeaker from the pool room jukebox. In late afternoon the dancers were all children; as the evening advanced, teenagers and adults joined in, so that by the time the party broke up, after eleven, adults predominated. (My little girls loved it: they went home in an "I could have danced all night" euphoria).

An age-grading, or lack of age-grading, system which lets children participate in the world of adults also allows biological adults to play the role of children to a considerable extent. There is no sharp dividing line between the world of the little boys who wander the streets of La Laja in the cool of the evening and the groups of men who gather to drink and talk at the little *abastos*. It is not felt to be shameful for a man in his twenties to be living with his mother, supported by her out of her earnings as a laundress.

Nor do parents in La Laja encourage autonomy in their children. There is practically no way for children to earn money in La Laja, but if there were, I do not believe that parents would want to see their children in a position to acquire spending money on their own. The American father's pride in his son's "newspaper route" would be incomprehensible to parents who, if conscientious about their children, want to keep the young under their control as much as possible.

Parents in La Laja do not characteristically try to develop moral automony in their children. When they discipline them, they generally do so physically—and this can mean some rather rough handling; I have seen children badly bruised from disciplinary beatings—without accompanying the punishment by the sort of verbal shaming and guilt-attributing designed to make the child internalize the prohibition.

It seems likely that the processes of social mobility will be facilitated if adults develop appropriate new styles of child rearing and that the focus of child rearing appropriate for one jump in stage is not necessarily that appropriate to another.

At the levels at which children are being brought up to try to satisfy their wants—traditional ones or new ones—through fairly traditional skills, it may work perfectly well to focus the discipline of children on seeing that they do not annoy or interfere with adults. Children, then, are punished for stealing or breaking adults' property, for failing to do a bit of assigned housework, for disturbing adults in some way. Outside those areas in which the actions of the child concern the adults directly, the child can do pretty much as he pleases. Why not? The child will never have to take more than the most superficial sort of cues from individuals who are socially distant from him; most of what he learns he will learn from people to whom he can easily relate as peers or near peers.

When the focus of mobility comes to be the enactment of a different sort of social role, it becomes necessary for children to learn to present themselves in more deliberately stylized ways. People have to learn to practice behavior in dress and manner which may be uncongenial to them as individuals and to cue themselves as to those behaviors by responding to the proper adult models "out there." At this point it is appropriate to have parents try to exert a general control over their children, to see that they stay clean, are consistently polite, do not roam about too much or too freely with their peers, and pay attention to teachers as they will later have to pay attention to supervisors.

These are, of course, not the only possible variants of child-rearing focus. The behavior of part of the American middle class, for example, suggests that it is possible to bring up children in a fairly subtle combination of pressure for autonomy and for high sensitivity to social cues, which will make it possible for the individual to groom himself for social roles in time and social distance quite far from him.

At this point, however, such a child-training focus is very far off the horizon for the people of La Laja. It is only remarkable that in La Laja those adults who have gained a moderately secure toe-hold in the system through a secure job in one of "the companies" generally show, so much and so quickly, a tendency to translate their life situation into styles of child rearing which will tend to fit their children for even neater adaptation to that world. These are the parents who insist that their small children stay clean, that they act "respectful," that they stay as much as possible under adult control; some of these parents send their children to private school because they say the atmosphere there is "more orderly" than in public school.

It thus comes about, interestingly enough, that a distinction which appears to be emerging in La Laja between two levels within the *clase obrero* is expressed as strongly in the style of child rearing as it is in anything else. While the more economically established, thrift-practicing families tend, not unnaturally, to have somewhat better-furnished homes than others, there is so far no such clear difference in style of self-presentation as that which at one time made Americans speak of the "shanty Irish" as against the "lace curtain Irish." As in the United States there is a tendency for the difference in life-style, as expressed in saving, long-term planning and control of children, to be associated with differences in family structure—stable "family circle" versus female-based family with males marginal. But this association would not appear to be crucial. Indeed, one of the families "of respect" in La Laja which has been most successful in rearing young people to fit into the new economic order—one son from this family plans to study accounting in Canada—is headed by a woman who may be said to be practicing "respect" behavior by remaining single. In another case I knew well, it was precisely a growing gulf of class difference which split a family and produced a female-headed, mobility-oriented unit.

When I first knew Maria, she was living in La Laja with her husband and five children, from ten to one year in age. Maria's husband, seventeen years older than Maria, was a smiling, slow-spoken man, much respected in the community and active in such communal matters as the building of the water line. He could neither read nor write; he spent his time running a little shop, where he was to be seen all day long dressed in pants and undershirt beaming amiably from behind the counter below a hanging fringe of cobwebbed eggbeaters and stalks of plantains. Maria's parents lived in the house just behind hers. They had been among the very first settlers in the barrio. They were also both illiterate.

Maria, on the other hand, had completed the sixth grade in the school of the Iron Mines Company. More than that, since she was a bright and attractive girl, the doctors and nurses of the Iron Mines dispensary had taken a fancy to her and had taught her nursing. They had even offered to send her to nursing school. "But then," says Maria, "I got married."

In working-class Venezuela, however, a woman is not required or expected to submerge her personality into the role of mother and housewife. Maria was still bright and attractive, and she continued to make friends—not only in the barrio where she was active in organizing community affairs, but in town. When the Social Security hospital opened up, Maria immediately got a job there as a nurse. She used the resulting income and social contacts with great effectiveness. Maria put two girls in private school and talked about sending the eldest of these—a child with much of the mother's charm, intelligence, and poise—to secretarial school in

Trinidad. (English is important for fitting oneself for a white-collar job with "the companies.") Maria took classes in embroidery and fancywork in San Félix which helped to put her in contact with women more definitely middle-class in style. She would make social calls in the evening, accompanied by the two youngest little boys, dressed in starched suits. When Maria's youngest child was baptized in church, the announcement cards listed as honorary godparents a school teacher, several beauticians, and several doc-tors.

Still living in La Laja, still in the house next to the shop with the hanging plantains and rusty eggbeaters, Maria gave a birthday party for one of the children which filled the little street of La Laja with the parked cars of the guests, many of whom were nurses and technicians (although no full-fledged doctors) from the hospital. Maria's parents were both at the party also. It all seemed to me no small thing to have achieved. I thought that it would have been very hard in the United States to achieve a similar upward mobili-ty without severing oneself from one's nonmobile kin.

Eventually, however, the strain was too much. Relations be-tween Maria and her husband became so bad that for weeks they were not on speaking terms. Maria's husband said that Maria was being unfaithful to him. Maria said that he was nothing but a "*bruto*"—an uncultured man. Still remaining on very close terms with her parents, Maria moved out of La Laja and began dickering with the development agency for a little house in one of the new urbanizations in which people of the life-style Maria was trying to achieve were living, not intermixed with other class elements.

When I left and lost connection with Maria, it was still too early to tell how it would come out for her and her children. Things had not been going well. Maria had been unable to get one of the houses in the new urbanization and was living either with her parents or in a rented house in a "barrio *bajo*" much like La Laja. More serious, she had been undergoing a lengthy series of operations which not only undercut the economic basis of her effort but also made it impossible for her to give her children proper supervision; the little girl who, it was hoped, would study in Trinidad and get a job eventually as secretary "with the company," looked strained and unwell and had been missing school. Maria still hoped to finish with the operations, go back to work at the hospital, and reorganize her life and that of her children.

Until recently, all ways up for people like the residents of La Laja have been through "the companies." They have been the source of the income which could be translated into change of life-style; they have served as technical schools—"It was like a school; no one knew how to do the work when they came, but the company would put someone with experience to show how"; they have also been sources of personal career guidance and sponsorship. One working man in La Laja claims that Americans are particularly good as teachers. According to him, Venezuelan bosses just like to "command," but without following through; Italians try to keep the technical know-how to themselves; but Americans really like to teach the workers. It does seem to be true in a number of cases that individuals have been helped over extended periods by developing a relationship in one of the "companies" with some individual who has served as tutor and sponsor. The young man of La Laja who works in the Orinoco Mining Company office and who is planning to study accounting in Canada lives with relatives of one of his American supervisors. A Venezuelan couple, now thoroughly middle-class in white-collar job and life-style, who live in the Iron Mines camp, go every year to place flowers on the grave of the American who served *them* as such a sponsor and teacher.

To climb the upward ladders presented by "the companies," formal education used not to be crucial; there was such a shortage of people with the formal educational attainments that a steady man who could learn could move up without them. Alberto, who had a well-paying job as a mechanic with Iron Mines, had a third-grade education; Pablo, who had a responsible job on the steel mill dock, had been through fourth grade; Marcos, who as a bachelor with a responsible job on the Iron Mines water system had one of the best houses in La Laja, had only a first-grade education; and Jorge, an electrician at the steel plant, had only been through second grade.

Jorge was born forty years ago in the delta of the Orinoco. His parents had a small farm there, growing cacao and sugar cane. Neither could read or write. His two living brothers and one of his two living sisters are still in the delta, the men still farmers; the other sister is married and lives in San Félix. Jorge went to school intermittently and worked on the farm; he had managed to complete second grade by the time he left school for good at fifteen. He would have liked to go on studying but "there was no possibility." At fifteen he became a *commerciante*—a petty trader—in the delta capital of Tucupita, and he made a living as a vendor of agricultural produce for nine years.

Then when Jorge was twenty-four he decided to see what he

could do up the river, where jobs were opening up around the establishing Iron Mines Company in San Félix. Jorge came directly to La Laja and stayed with a friend who already had a job with the Iron Mines Company. (Fifteen years later he still lives in La Laja and still works for Iron Mines, by now in a foreman's position.) Jorge, too, got a job as laborer with Iron Mines. The Company laid him off after seven years, but it had been seven years well spent; he came to the company as a laborer, and he left it an electrician. It had all been on-the-job training. "The boss liked me," says Jorge, "and he showed me how."

After the company, there was a year out of work, but then Jorge went to work as an electrical repairman in an electrical store in San Félix. There were two years at that. Jorge was proud of being an electrician, but dissatisfied at the rate of pay; in 1960 he tried again, with a small grocery store, to be a businessman. This was not successful financially either, so it was a distinct step up when in 1962 he succeeded in getting a job as an electrician in the new steel mill. In 1963 the steel mill reclassified him at a higher level; in 1964 he became a *"jefe de turno"* or foreman; in 1965 he got another raise.

Meanwhile, in the way which seems to be characteristic of the people of La Laja, he continued to try to put savings into "mounting a business." Since Jorge still owned a house in La Laja, and since he was able to buy a liquor license from another resident of the barrio who had never been able to muster the capital to put it to use, he began to collaborate with his wife and her brother in starting a bar—that bar which was to become the continual purveyor of very cold beer and very loud music across the street from us and which figures in some remarks on La Laja's commercial economy earlier in this account.

Meanwhile, Jorge's son completed primary school, started in high school, and began to dabble—with no very conspicuous success—at founding a small bicycle repair business back of the bar.

Jorge is proud of his job and proud of how far he has come. He believes that the most important thing the president of Venezuela could do for people like himself is to "promote industry so that everyone may work." But he still looks for security in having a business of his own; if he had a lot of capital, he says, what he would like to do with it is to start his own business in electrical appliances and electrical repairs.

He reads the papers every day, following especially the international news. In 1965, when asked what news he had read recently had struck him as most interesting, he at once cited that about the space capsule, Gemini 5.

In the same way, fifty-three-year-old Pablo, who had a relatively well-paying job on the dock at the steel mill, had learned his technical skills all on various jobs he had held since he left school with a fourth-grade education. Pablo had been a sailor, had worked for the oil companies, and had worked for the Iron Mines Company for ten years before he went to the steel plant. He, too, would like to be in business for himself; if he were to get a large sum of money, he says, he would like to "start an industry to make something." In the meantime he had been able to invest his savings and terminal pay from various jobs in building four houses. (It happens in La Laja that the social system often taxes the successful; one house was occupied by an unemployed friend who was to pay "what he could" and another by his wife's relatives, rent-free; one was left for commercial renting. Pablo had also loaned 8000 bolívares of his savings to help set up a nephew in a radio and television repair business in Puerto La Cruz.)

In the meantime, Pablo, more than Jorge, focused on his children as a way of consolidating his gains. Pablo and his wife were investing also in their children's education; the eldest boy was going to the technical school, and second child attending the nuns' school in San Félix. They had 15,000 bolívares in the bank for the children's education. "That's what I'm working for," Pablo says to his children, "so you won't grow up *bruto*." I asked twelve-year-old José what he would like to be when he grows up. "A doctor." "A medical doctor?" "Yes, or an engineer." José has no very clear idea how one gets to be either of these things, it appears. His parents do not either, but meanwhile his father gives José money for pencils, and Pablo's wife flashes her ravishing smile and irons her daughter's school uniform and sees that the children get off for school in the morning.

When La Laja (as the result of the sewer controversy) elected a new *junta comunal* for the barrio, the vice-president was twenty-three-year-old Leonardo, who had been living in the barrio less than a year with his wife and small daughter. His election, probably more than in the case of any of the other junta members, was a tribute to clear technical expertise. Leonardo could type and keep books, he spoke very competent English, and he drove his new Volkswagen every day to a bookkeeper's job at the Guri dam site.

Leonardo's father was in the Guardia Nacional and, although not well-off, made it possible for Leonardo to get through primary school in the little town of Puerto Ayacucho where he grew up, downriver from San Félix. Leonardo left school at fourteen. He would have liked to have continued. He went to work as an errand boy, and it was as such that he began to work in San Félix when he came there with his family at the age of fifteen. The professional turning point for him seems to have been when he got a job as office boy in the CVG camp. That helped him to get a similar job with a construction company in town, and in the construction company he met people who interested themselves in him and helped and encouraged him to spend two years studying in Trinidad, where he learned English, bookkeeping, and typing. When he came back he was put in charge of the construction company office.

Since then, he has had a number of different jobs; in all cases but one he terminated each of his own volition to get a better one. He bought a substantial house in La Laja, and he traded in his Volkswagen for a more expensive vehicle. He, like Maria, intends to move from La Laja to one of the new urbanizations if he can manage it; he says he does not want his children to grow up with the "disorderly" people who are his neighbors in La Laja.

Leonardo, more than any one else I knew in La Laja, had developed that style of life which we call middle-class in its emphasis on individual self-control as the basis of dominance. Where other people, when asked what individuals like themselves could do to solve the problems of the country, expressed impotence ("nothing· without money"), or proposed group action (Pablo says "call a congress to get the people behind an idea"), Leonardo finds his contribution to the nation's problems in "telling and showing friends the best way to live, saving money, having a small family, avoiding troubles."

Leonardo might be thought to have attained success, or at least, the basis of success. He does not think so. He has gone back to school, intending to get a *bachillerato* by studying at night. Leonardo says that it used to be true that a man could succeed if he had the intelligence and desire to do so just by working his way up in the companies. Soon, he says, this will not be possible. Soon, if you do not have the diploma, you will not be able to get the job. He intends to be ready with the diploma.

If Leonardo is right—and it seems likely that he is—there will be an added premium on being brought up in the right family now. What will happen to the six boys of Emma, who lived across the street from me, and used to send over her children to ask for a "small loan" to buy bread or powdered milk? The oldest son, aged twenty, with a second-grade education, was working a half week as laborer at the steel mill. The sixteen-year-old was illiterate, and the younger boys ran around in dirty shorts and did not go to school. When they got evicted for nonpayment of rent, the development corporation helped Emma get a lot in a new low-income urbanization at the other side of San Félix. But no one could seem to help Emma find the money to build a house or even to pay the rent on the lot, and in the new urbanization the boys still did not go to school—indeed, the school there had not been built.

11.
Social Process and
Economic Development

The business of daily life in La Laja, with its occasional peaks and crises, might be looked at in a number of ways. Human life on a small scale has an intrinsic human interest, as the phenomenon of small town gossip attests. Beyond that one may try to analyze the happenings in one small community to develop some more general notions as to the nature of social and cultural processes in other similar communities; anthropologists have made a profession based largely on this sort of analysis. The business of life in La Laja may be thought of as having a particular interest in reflecting the violent and uneven social and economic transformation of a nation, a transformation which, in turn, may be generalized as one instance of a general class of transformations making up the major move-ment of modern history. But to say that events in La Laja reflect a general process of national development may be taken in more than one way. One might think of these events as results of a process of development, as sparks thrown off from a machinery in rapid operation. Or one might think of them as the very process itself, when it is broken down into its smallest instances.

The second point of view is adopted here. For the text of my examination of life in La Laja in this context, I might take the words of Hla Myint ("An Interpretation of Economic Backwardness"; A. N. Agarwala and S. P. Singh, *The Economics of Underdevelopment*, New York: Oxford University Press, 1963):

> There is then a greater need in the study of backward countries than in that of the advanced countries to go behind the veil of conventional social accounting into the real processes of adaptation between wants, activities and environment which we have described earlier on as the "economic struggle." When we do this we shall see that the "problem" of the backward countries as it is commonly discussed really has two distinct aspects: on the subjective side it might be described as the economics of discontent and maladjustment; on the objective side it might be described as the economics of stagnation, low *per capita* productivity and incomes.

This point of view requires us to conceive of economic processes as a good deal more than technical and financial. It requires us to conceive of economic institutions as having their social and cultural aspects, and as being related to other social and political institutions in a complex structure. This is, by now, not a novel point of view.

We have, in the developed societies, created an institutional technology, a set of institutions capable not only of managing the tools and machinery and of producing and distributing the goods and services, but of generating new forms of tools and machinery and even developing new institutions at an accelerating rate. The "economic" institutions are closely involved with the "social" or "political" ones. As illustration, one might consider what is involved in our system of taxation, or note that an American economist writes about "countervailing power," referring to institutions which are perhaps even more political than economic.

The gap between the rich and the poor nations, the "developed" and the "underdeveloped," is reflected in such economic indicators as production and per capita income figures, but the standard indicators merely point to and imperfectly represent the crucial differences which are those of structure. The "haves" among nations are not just richer; they are rich because they have developed the institutions which make them rich, and which are perpetually tending to make them richer still. The gap is not easily closed even by providing the backward nations with compensating increments of capital and technical advice from the developed ones, since the institutional differences mean that the backward countries are less able to make effective use of these increments than the developed nations can of their capital and technique. The central problem of development appears to be that of using such increments of capital and technical advice in ways which will enable the backward nations to develop the appropriate institutions for modern economic activity. Since these institutions are social and political as well as economic, the problem of economic development comes to be seen, in general, as a problem of broad social transformation, and in each particular instance, as analyzable only in terms of a particular structure of institutions.

In this view, it also becomes relevant to note that the various nations, to the extent that they are following a single path of historical development, are following it not independently but together. The historical situation is crucially different for the backward countries of the present, because they are experiencing their backwardness in a world of already-developed nations. This has multiple consequences.

The developed nations can and do serve the backward nations as sources of capital and technical expertise. But this very relationship of leader to follower generates its own anguish. When the first comers were in the early stages of development, there were at least no already-developed neighbors with which to make comparison. Today the comparison is there for the members of the backward nations to see and envy, and the news is brought to the people of the backward nation by the means of mass communication which achieved technique makes possible. The people of the backward nations do not want merely to follow; they want to catch up. When they see their own economic progress in the context of a constant or increasing gulf between their own level and that of their success models, the comparison generates political pressures, both between and within nations, which may be difficult for political institutions to deal with.

Furthermore, economic development brings power, and the already-developed nations are, for the backward ones, competitors and dominators. There is a disparity of military and political power between the developed and the backward nations which is derived from and supported by the disparities of economic position.

Economic development of a backward country in a world of developed countries may take a classic form which is, from the technological point of view, the mine or plantation; from the political point of view, colonialism; from the economic point of view, the dual economy. The backward country which exists in a world of developed, capital-exporting, politically dominant nations experiences a sort of partial economic development, dominated by its relationship to the developed societies outside.

The backward country comes to have a "developed sector" of mines or plantations based on increments of foreign capital and dominated by foreign investors and managers; a large part of the society and economy continues on in traditional cultural and economic patterns, usually based on subsistence agriculture. The two sectors of the society and economy are only loosely connected. The developed sector produces mainly for export, the traditional sector mainly for direct consumption. Members of the backward sector leave their traditional communities to work for wages in the plantations or mines and bring into the traditional sector new consumption goods which they are able to buy with their wages. The "developed sector" is organized technologically to fit a society where few people have modern technical skills and there is a surplus of unskilled labor. It operates in a political and social context in which power and status are highly centralized, with the center of the system outside the backward country. Wage and promotion policies in the mines and plantations tend to reflect this situation, as well as the low productivity of labor, through a "cheap labor policy." There comes to be a sort of ethnic occupational status stratigraphy in which foreign managers dominate the technology at the top, being allied with a very small native elite; the "natives" form a large mass of unskilled and relatively vertically immobile labor at the bottom; and in between a group of middle-level technicians and entrepreneurs consists largely of foreign immigrants. The economic gains made within the developed sector tend to be drained out in paying for goods produced in the more developed nations, rather than to become the basis for a more general spread of economic development throughout the backward society.

Venezuela has approached this model several times in its history. The first was as a basically agricultural economy. The second was during the oil era, with the oilfields serving the role of the foreign-dominated developed sector within the backward society. Current national economic policy in Venezuela might be described most simply as an attempt to move the society away from the dual economy model, to redirect the economic gains of the developed sector back into the society in such a way as to make for a more generally distributed economic growth which will have greater potential for indigenous economic dynamism in the future.

But the institutions which this process must transform are a particular set of institutions, formed in the course of a particularly rich and glittering limited-sector development. The context for Venezuelan economic development is not simply that the economy is still highly dependent on a single, foreign-dominated oil sector, but also that this form of economic development has shaped the political and social institutions of Venezuela in certain ways. The dual economy, it might be said, has been internalized. Venezuela is not a plantation economy. But that model may serve to point to some ways in which Venezuela, with its cloverleaf highways and its travertine-faced apartment buildings is still a country developed only in part, and in which the partial nature of its development has been institutionalized. Oil wealth, coming into a country with a classically small and separate upper class, remade that local elite, but it also has given it a new basis for the elite position. The oil boom brought into Venezuela, as in the model, a group of middle-level technicians and entrepreneurs, and as in the model, they are still a group relatively separate in the social order, even though some Venezuelans have joined them. The localized nature of oil prosperity drew the unskilled "natives" into the cities, but they are still largely unskilled and less adapted for mobility than the urban working class of more developed nations.

In the classic "dual economy" the economic development in mining or plantations has a strong counterbalance in the "traditional way of life." People leave their villages to work in the mines or on the plantations, but their kinsmen and fellow community members remain behind, planting and harvesting and carrying on the rituals of communal life. The wage earner still has a connection to a life which will receive him when he returns. He goes forth to make money as the Indian in a hunting or raiding party may have gone forth to hunt or raid; his base is still in the traditional society.

In eastern Venezuela, the traditional, rural agricultural life was too weak economically and in terms of social organization to withstand the pull of the developed sector. The clearly inferior opportunities of the rural setting pushed people off the land as the glittering city drew them to it. The city did not offer any surety of employment, but the rural areas offered sure poverty. The *campesinos* poured into the cities and remained there as a large mass of unskilled, intermittently employed persons, committed to the cash economy but in a society which did not yet offer full participation to all its members. The dual society with exceptional rapidity became the bipolar society. La Laja, an urban neighborhood in which over 25 percent unemployment is normal, is a segment of such a bipolar society.

The very oil wealth which potentially gives Venezuela the chance of competing in a world of efficient producers by means of the most modern capital equipment meant that those into whose pockets oil put money to spend could satisfy their new wants with imported goods. This, in turn, meant that the new wealth was not translated, except in small part, into opportunities for local manufacturing, and thus for jobs.

Venezuela is not moving from small to larger to large as did England. Its development is like the dual-society models in involving the entrance of large capital organizations and already-complex technology into the otherwise backward society. Even when a Venezuelan-owned steel mill is added to the American-controlled oilfields and iron mines of the developed sector, the sharp gap between sectors still remains. The gap is not as conspicuous as it is in those partly developed societies where it is visually expressed in the contrast between rural and urban. In Venezuela, as the rural people move into the cities and adopt urban styles of dress and housing, the gap is concealed, as it were, by a kind of cultural disguise. But it is still there. It is built into the structure of the city. Furthermore, it seems likely that there are things about the economic development and urbanization process itself which tend to accentuate the gap rather than to close it.

The first of these characteristics is a high level of unemployment, the structural unemployment and concealed unemployment or underemployment which substitutes in Venezuela for the low-productivity rural employment of the model. Economic development impinges on the people of La Laja in the form of capital-intensive industry, providing a relatively small number of jobs with relatively high degrees of skill. In neither aspect do the jobs fit the job seekers, who are many and unskilled. So in La Laja it is the period of construction, the period when the companies were building their facilities, which is spoken of as the era of prosperity. That is when there were jobs for the unskilled, jobs which disappeared when the iron companies or the steel mill went into production. Pablo, who gets a regular income from his two rented houses in San Félix, used that period of opportunity for the unskilled to lift himself to a plateau of relative economic security which serves him now that men without skills are obsolete. Jorge, who worked his way up in the ranks to become an electrician, capitalized the gains of that stage in another way. But others were not so competent or so lucky, and at forty found themselves already economically obsolete. Their sons, if they do not make themselves into other kinds of people, will have the same experience. Many are now growing up on the fringes of an economy which does not want them, and in which they might—if things do not change fast enough—never find themselves in demand. They will, then, not serve the economy either, for they will be neither efficient producers nor a source of consumer demand for goods. The structural unemployment built into the present Venezuelan economy is a key factor in "the economics of discontent and maladjustment" as it is in, "the economics of stagnation, low per capita productivity and incomes."

Other consequences follow from the high level of structural unemployment; it is the center of social processes which intensify its primary effects. Human beings adjust themselves to the situation in which they live, whether it be in the Arctic tundra or a city in the interior of Venezuela where for an individual at any given time it is sure that everything will cost money, but the odds on being paid some money are not high. The human adjustment to this classic proletarian situation takes the form of short-term survival techniques, at best focusing on other people as the main source of security. For those people at the greatest disadvantage in the system, it takes the form of the "culture of poverty" described by Oscar Lewis, in which the scramble to keep going is so acute that even stable personal relationships become difficult to maintain. In such a social world the ad hoc arrangements for solving the problems of each day and deriving each day's immediate satisfactions come to dominate the cognitive field to a degree which makes long-range thinking and planning quite difficult. It becomes, in this context, even harder than the immediate practical difficulties would suggest for those young people of La Laja who are growing up obsolete to design and train themselves into something different.

A particular aspect of the "culture of poverty" is the kind of family structure which develops in response to the situation of life at the bottom of this kind of economy. The economic marginality of the man makes his position as a husband and father marginal also. The result is matrifocal or female-headed families which are, in the absence of jobs for women, even more vulnerable than those headed by unskilled men and even less able to serve as centers to train young people in the competences demanded by the new order.

It thus comes about that the very economic development which intends, in the long range, to close the gap between the "developed sector" and the "backward sector" at the same time creates a sort of backwash, a subsidiary set of processes which are of a kind to maintain the gap.

The oil and mining boom which produced the recently formed incipient middle class seen now in La Laja also produced social institutions which organized and protected that group's interests, in such a way as to put those who failed to get into the system at a cumulative disadvantage in now making the jump upward. Part of the process by which Venezuela digested the foreign-owned oil enterprises was the mobilizing of a good deal of what might be called, in an extension of Galbraith's use of the term, "countervailing power." On the national scale this took the form of tapping the oil companies for national revenue used, in part, for job-creating public works programs and currently serving as the basis of the industrial development effort. It also took the form of a structure of legal regulations and of collective bargaining institutions which ensure that the level of wages and fringe benefits provided to workers in the big companies will be quite high. The established worker in a big company has not only wages and housing allowances, but medical care (which is both free and generally superior to that available outside), schools, and school supplies. Those who have gotten a place in the developed sector not only have, individually, more resources for establishing their children and helping them to move upward in the system, but also are provided directly by the system with assistance in that direction.

Those outside are at a competitive disadvantage from every point of view. Economically, they are marginal and insecure. They lack access to social services at the same level as their more fortunate compatriots. Politically, they suffer from the disadvantage experienced in the United States by such unorganized groups as the migrant farm workers, when the labor movement had established itself as a political force so effectively as to lose interest in extending its organizational base. None of the Venezuelan political parties, from left to right, is at present seriously involved in organizing this group at the bottom. Thus, the structure of the political institutions contributes to the gap shaped by the structure of the economy and the "culture of poverty" which reflects that structure.

The people of La Laja are not, like the unskilled workers of the plantation-economy model, confronting a social order in which the social gap between "worker" and "manager" is so great that it is almost inconceivable—and close to impossible—for an individual at the bottom to hurdle it. In La Laja is to be seen an incipient middle class so recently formed, and still so close to its origins, that those who have not made the jump can see before them persons with whom they can easily identify who have made it. A single group of kinsmen may include both sorts of individuals. And one can still make the jump from "backward sector" of the society to "developed" and developing.

But a consideration of the situation suggests that it may be getting harder. The very process of urban development and the growth of urban institutions may well be making it harder. Now that secondary education is becoming more available, now that the technical school has opened its doors and some people are beginning to attend it, there is appearing a new source of differentiation, a new hurdle to jump. As the accountant who lives in La Laja told me, "Pretty soon you won't be able to get a job without education and get trained by the company; you will have to have the diploma." This young man sees what has to be done, and he is doing it by going to school at night. Many others are not. As the city grows, its neighborhoods become differentiated by social class. The planners in Caracas are contributing to this natural process; each little "urbanization" is projected for a certain income range. The young accountant and the nurse in La Laja want to move to some "better neighborhood," and as such neighborhoods develop, they will be able to do so. In a few years the people of La Laja may lose their sort of leadership—and both these people have been important leaders in the barrio, as well as potential social models.

Just as what Myint calls "disequalizing factors" may perpetuate for many years in the colonial plantation economy a "developed sector" next to a "backward sector," so within a single national economy there may be disequalizing factors which tend to perpetuate such a development gap. In the foregoing I have tried to point to such disequalizing factors as the view from the barrio exposes them. This is not to say that economic development is frozen. Economic development and social change are taking place in Venezuela rapidly. Living in La Laja I was very aware of this; it was the stuff of which daily life was made. The people of La Laja were aware of it too; they talked of *"el futuro del pais"* (the nation's future) and of how the city was changing year by year and month by month. But those disequalizing factors which are, in the long run, impediments to continuing economic and social transformation are there, even if general observation of change and aggregate statistics of development leave them out of account. Even if the forces for change are stronger than they are, the factors which impede development are worth considering in a society which may well need to bring about economic development very rapidly indeed.

It has been pointed out that the process of economic development tends by its very nature to be an uneven one. Hirschman, in particular, has suggested that the imbalances and inequalities which arise in the course of economic development are some of the major sorts of stimuli for further development, as people are motivated to see that the backward sectors "catch up." But for imbalances to act as a stimulus requires that they be reflected in pressures for new development, either through the market, or through social and political institutions. There is no reason to believe that the process of pressure formation will operate in any more automatically balancing fashion than the economic process itself.

In considering the possible consequences of lengthy perpetuation of the gap between the two parts of the polarized society, it should be noted that "discontent and maladjustment" are to some extent separable from "stagnation, low per capita productivity and incomes." Discontent is built on claims unsatisfied; it rests on hope and aspiration as much as on lack of satisfaction. Those who cannot imagine better cannot feel deprived, even though they may be unhappy. A society which has, like Venezuela, high rates of urbanization and thriving mass communications, combined with a very high level of structural unemployment, is bound to generate some sorts of dissatisfaction at the bottom of the society among the people who learn to want all sorts of things which they have no effective way of getting. A sizable gap between wanting and getting may be called, by definition, a maladjustment. But even those sorts of discontents and maladjustments may not appear directly as a social problem of a serious nature. To call a situation a "problem" implies some social definition as to the problematic. Even an unemployment rate averaging 17 percent of the nonagricultural active population is not a "national problem" unless it is so defined; without such a social definition it is the problem only of the people who are unemployed. If their individual discontents and maladjustments are never aggregated and organized in political institutions, they may demand to be coped with by society merely as they emerge indirectly in other recognized problem areas. Venezuelan politics may eventually develop ways of aggregating and organizing the discontents at the bottom, but so far there is little in that direction. A survey made in Ciudad Guayana during my stay showed nine-tenths of the unskilled workers regarding any position in Venezuelan society as accessible to any capable person, and nine-tenths regarding their life as happy and expecting the future to be better still. This suggests that the people at the bottom are still far from conceiving of their situation as one calling for "social protest." Although the "problem of unemployment" figures in the rhetoric of politics, and the reduction of unemployment is stated as a major objective of national planning, none of the political parties has yet developed the kind of mass base among the unemployed or marginally employed which would use their situation as a lever for change. The Venezuelan labor movement operates frankly as a special interest group very far from the sort of labor politics which gave the United States a slogan: "Sixty Million Jobs."

A set of "countervailing institutions" which represented the group at the bottom might no doubt be dangerous to social stability and would at least be troublesome and inconvenient, for it would define the structure of the economy as "a problem" for political economy to solve. In giving the discontents of the people at the bottom institutional expression, they would tend to generate a sense of problem, to aggregate and aggravate dissatisfactions. But such "countervailing institutions" might be useful as well.

If Venezuela is to continue to move away from the dual economy model, it is those people at the bottom, that "backward sector," who must be drawn into the development process. Serious stickiness in development comes out of the vested interests of those groups who have already established places in the social-economic system in its underdeveloped or partly developed form; this is true both of the gap between "developed" and "backward" nations, and of gaps between sectors within nations. The social and political institutions which push change forward are often those which represent the groups of disadvantaged, pressuring now for their place at the table. One of the problems of economic development in the "backward countries" is that insofar as it is deliberately planned and organized, the planners and organizers are usually those of relatively high social position who, while perhaps thoroughly committed to economic growth, are in a position to feel realistically uneasy about social change. It is not only practically easier, it is psychologically more attractive, for them to project economic development in terms of aggregate statistics and large, capital-intensive projects.

Even if the appropriate political leverage were to be mobilized to tackle the problem of the "disequalizing factors" head on, it is not an easy problem to tackle. The problem is not dissimilar from the "poverty problem" in the United States, for which we are now mounting a considerable national effort but for which we are still—even in our much less extreme case—far from developing an adequate long-range strategy.

In general, I suppose there are two broad sorts of strategies which would have to be tried in conjunction and coordination. One is the reduction of structural unemployment through promoting and developing economic activities with a higher ratio of jobs to capital and which offer prospects of training the unskilled. The other general approach would be a variety of tactics for keeping open the connections across the gap, the channels of communication and mobility. These two strategies are at many points reciprocally interdependent. Neither is easy to accomplish.

Some ways of bridging the gap are fairly obvious. National policy in the field of education could be to provide not only schools for all, as is the policy of the Venezuelan government now, but the books, buses, school lunches, and scholarships which make it possible for even the child of the unemployed worker or the child without a father to stay in school and learn. Even such fairly obvious measures would appear as a massive national effort. The schools could have attached to them a series of tutorial and guidance services, perhaps suggested by the "homework clinics," "tutoring programs," and "guidance counselors" with which the United States has been experimenting, but adapted to Venezuelan conditions;·the aim of these would be to help young people to grow up fast and effectively into a world in which skills are needed and for which their own parents can have no basis of experience to prepare them. For adults beyond the school age, Venezuela might need to develop a national employment service of a flexibility and sophistication far beyond that of the United States; the claims on it would be far greater. In Ciudad Guayana, specifically, there could be an attempt to keep the models of success available to the unsuccessful by promoting residential heterogeneity—and this is not easy, either, for while such is, in theory, the planners' policy now, practice tends to be one of separating, because of the problems of designing and building a block or a neighborhood in which some people can pay for services which others cannot afford. To some extent there can be an effort to support and promote the social and political institutions which connect the individuals of the levels below with those above. We say that there can be such an effort, and we may agree that there should be—but this is something which we still have few technical prescriptions for accomplishing; here planning moves clearly into the painful processes of politics.

There is very little use, and considerable danger, in grooming people for upward mobility if there are not slots into which they can move. The mobility strategy thus depends on at least moderate success in an economic strategy—a strategy for rather rapidly reducing the high structural unemployment in Venezuela. Of course, although capital-intensive, primary industry also tends to generate secondary industries and other jobs, the situation of Venezuela seems to suggest a national effort focused directly on producing more jobs faster. Venezuela seems to need, and quite soon, many economic activities with a fairly high ratio of jobs to capital. That is not so easy, either. Such activities are probably in themselves harder to promote, particularly in a nation which has a good deal of capital but in which administrative machinery is still underdeveloped. In addition, in Venezuela, they have to survive with a very strong labor movement, where wages are maintained at a fairly high level in established industries, and where the general level of worker skill is not high. Venezuela is also a country with a high cost of living and high consumer aspirations. People left the farms because it is more attractive to live in hope in the cities than in penury on the land. The jobs have to pay off in that context.

"Cottage industries" find it hard to compete in a marketplace where Japanese plastics sell in quantity; the earnings from such industries do not look attractive to people who keep hoping to get a job at the steel mill or the Orinoco Mining Company. Developing agriculture looks like a rational strategy in a country which is simultaneously importing food at high prices and finding it hard to handle the rate of migration from farm to city. But talking to the people still in agriculture, either on small individual farms or on the settlements of the land reform program, makes it clear that they, too, have opted for the new world; they will not stay on the land unless life on the land comes with schools, clinics, and other "urban" amenities. We do not yet know enough about the technical possibilities of agriculture in the area to know whether farm production can be made to support the amenities; if not, people can be held on the land only by a rather high rate of subsidy. Perhaps a labor-intensive agriculture can be developed which will pay off; if not, it might be as well to carry those people in the cities, and make agriculture another capital-intensive industry. "Public works" is a classic strategem for making jobs, but it is a strategem better suited to temporary unemployment problems than to structural problems such as those of Venezuela. Besides, even "public works" is not an all-solving job producer in a country in which roads are built by heavy machinery rather than by the pick and shovel and in which, as mentioned earlier, my neighbors, laying a water line which they badly wanted, continually grumbled, "There are machines which could be digging this ditch ..." and left the main pick-and-shovel work to the very old and very young. Even public works in Venezuela is capital-intensive.

A country in the position of Venezuela must be continually improvising solutions to the immediate problems brought about by the rapidity of its own development. The Caracas public works program of the dictatorship was such an improvised solution to the problem of the urban migration. It had its horrors, but as a way of providing jobs in a hurry it also had its merits. But often the short-term measures accelerate the process of development and with the acceleration bring need for further solutions. So the Caracas public works program accelerated the urban growth to which it was a response. The planning of Ciudad Guayana was, in part, a response to the socially and politically explosive growth of Caracas, and the development of Ciudad Guayana has drawn still more rural Venezuelans into the turbulent stream of urban industrial life.

Venezuela has the capital resources and the relatively open social structure to do, in national development, what few other countries can do. But that very set of advantages is also a possible source of danger. A country like Venezuela lives in hope and optimism, but also in jeopardy. Its situation is that of a moving disequilibrium. It can no more stop or go backward than can a boy going downhill on a bicycle with his feet on the handlebars. The young people of La Laja are growing up in a world of schools and newspapers and movies, hair curlers, automobiles, and transistor radios. One can imagine them becoming many sorts of people, but it is not possible to conceive of them becoming *campesinos* like their grandparents. They are committed to the world of which those things are a part. Development has to create a society with places for them, or run the risk that, finding none, they will explode the society which has failed their very high expectations.

It might be possible through deliberate action to short-cut history even more than current policies imply. Development planning could take as its goal that of making places for everyone and helping everyone to take his place. This would mean promoting a very broad spectrum of economic activities—small manufactures as well as big ones, commerce as well as industry, modernized agriculture as well as urban occupations—and of creating, through an immense national effort in the field of general and technical education, the skills to fit people for the jobs. It would be an extraordinary achievement. The instances in history where nations have done anything of the sort suggest that to do it a nation needs particularly catalytic social and political institutions focused by some "revolutionary" ideology. I do not know whether Venezuela could do it. Perhaps even without such a violent transformation by deliberate national effort, transformation will come fast enough.

In any case, planned or unplanned, life in La Laja is part of an historic transformation. The intellectuals call it "economic development," but the people of La Laja may be on the right track when they speak of making the future, not with that dry technicians' phrase, but as *"haciendo patria"* (nation-making) and *"haciendo pueblo"* (making a people).

Index

ACCION 14, 63-65, 75, 79

Agriculture and livestock
  and education in rural areas 96
  and traditional knowledge in rural
    areas 107
  and urbanization 118, 125, 134
  and Venezuelan economy 22, 31,
    133
  as small business 27, 31-32, 57
  S. Figueres 95
  see also Migration

Aspirations
  and chance 100, 104
  and housing 17, 102, 117, 129, 141
  and marriage styles 46, 123-25
  and national development 24, 142
  and religious practices 114-16
  of lower class in La Laja 26, 39
  of migrants to La Laja 21, 28
  of unskilled workers in Ciudad
    Guayana 25
  of upper class in San Félix 12, 25
  transformation of 5-6, 21, 24-25, 32,
    39, 100, 104, 108, 122, 143
  values("respect") 57, 61, 95, 104,
    111, 123
  see also Education, as a goal; and
    Politics

Businesses
  and communications network 56
  as a form of savings 38, 126
  in Ciudad Guayana 9-10, 34, 36-38
  in La Laja 27, 35-37
  rental housing 37
  see also Agriculture, as small
    business

Church
  Catholic 3, 9, 109, 113

Protestant 56, 105, 108, 113-17

Ciudad Guayana
  Puerto Ordaz 8, 10, 95
  San Félix 8-12, 20-27, 29, 58,
    69-70, 72-73, 75, 81, 96, 109,
    125, 127-28

Community development
  and public services 14, 29, 66-69
  and social controls 58-61
  and surplus labor 69
  around the issue of the sewer 75-77
  by residents of La Laja 14, 54-55,
    66-67, 74
  community center 14, 65-66
  in San Félix 70
  personalismo 62
  sense of community 9, 57, 73
  see also ACCION; CORDIPLAN;
    Companies, camps; Politics; and
    Underdevelopment and economic
    development process

Compadrazgo 41, 49, 55-56

Companies
  and businesses 9, 28, 37-38, 135
  as represented in La Laja 11
  as source of education 10, 23-24,
    28, 109, 111, 124-27
  as source of housing 10-11, 82, 129
  camps 10-11, 23-24, 27-28, 35, 74,
    95, 125
  developed sector of economy 34,
    122, 133
  require English 124
  see also Corporación Venezolana de
    Guayana, Mining companies, and
    Oil companies

CORDIPLAN 14, 63-66, 68

Corporación Venezolana de
  Guayana(CVG)

Selected Ann Arbor Paperbacks
Works of enduring merit

For a complete list of Ann Arbor Paperback titles write:
THE UNIVERSITY OF MICHIGAN PRESS ANN ARBOR